sex in design

TECIUM
PUBLISHERS

sex in design

© 2007 Tectum Publishers
Godefriduskaai 22
2000 Antwerp, Belgium
info@tectum.be
+32 3 2266673
www.tectum.be

ISBN: 90-76886-40-7
EAN: 9789076886404
(37) 2007/9021/4

Editorial Coordination: Anja Llorella Oriol

Text: Lou Andrea Savoir

Copy Editing: Barbara Burani

Art Direction & Graphic Design: Emma Termes Parera

French Translation: Olivier Fleuraud

Dutch Translation: Karolien Willems

Editorial project:
maomao publications
Tallers, 22, 3º 1ª
08001 Barcelona, Spain
Tel.: +34 93 481 57 22
Fax: +34 93 317 42 08
E-mail: mao@maomaopublications.com
Web site: www.maomaopublications.com

What is there to be afraid of?

Sex is interesting to everybody because everybody does it. Royalty, politicians, religious dignitaries, artists, neighbors, co-workers, your children, your parents, and yes, your ex. Sex is not considered innocent, and why should it be? If you're not having it, you wish you were, and either way, you envision it, question it, and feel strongly about it. Designers go through a similar process in regards to their work.

Sex and design is a winning combination. Sex's fun connotations actually lighten up the idea of design, which is often perceived as being elitist. Rich or poor, wherever you are from, you have sex. You experience it first hand, and so your opinions about it feel legitimate. Everybody can understand sex in design, or design that is sexual, no matter how abstracted. Abstracted: an elaborate take on a concrete idea, in this case sexual. Everybody is capable of having a dirty mind, which is what an elaborate take on a sexualized idea is often called.

This book is about good dirty ideas: sex and design in a relationship that goes beyond the vulgar breast-shaped corkscrew, or manufacturing the perpetual penis-shaped noodles. Design and sex are both informed by emotional, socio-cultural and visual factors, the reason why they are so popular when combined is that all of these factors become naturally enjoyable, reclaimed by the multitude. Sexual design tends to be inclusive rather then exclusive.

What we have here is an exceptionally loaded and diverse collection of work. The designers addressed each piece in a conscious manner. The sexual content makes for graspable design, and the design aspect fosters an imaginative, or reflexive approach towards the sexual. Sex and design can enrich one another.

Il n'y a pas de quoi avoir peur

Le sexe intéresse tout le monde car tout le monde couche. Têtes couronnées, politiciens, dignitaires religieux, artistes, voisins, collègues de travail, vos enfants, vos parents, et, oui, votre ex aussi. Le sexe n'est pas considéré de manière innocente, et c'est tout naturel. Si vous n'avez pas de relations sexuelles, vous rêvez d'en avoir; dans tous les cas, c'est un sujet d'imagination, de questionnement, un sujet qui vous tient à coeur. Les designers vivent un processus similaire dans leur travail.

Sexe et design forment un duo gagnant. Les connotations légères associées au sexe soulagent le design de son image souvent élitiste. Riche ou pauvre, quelles que soient vos origines, vous couchez. Vous en faites vous-même l'expérience, donc vous vous sentez légitime dans vos opinions sur le sujet. Tout le monde peut comprendre le sexe dans le design, ou le design sexué, aussi abstrait soit-il. Abstrait : un point de vue élaboré sur un sujet concret, en ce qui nous concerne, le sexe. Tout le monde est capable d'avoir les idées mal placées, et on dit souvent d'une idée élaborée à propos d'un sujet sexué qu'elle est mal placée.

Ce livre présente de bons exemples d'idées mal placées, qui associent sexe et design de manière plus intéressante que le vulgaire tire-bouchons « gros lolos » ou des sempiternelles « nouilles quéquettes ». Sexe et design sont tous deux fondés sur des facteurs émotionnels, socioculturels et visuels. Leur combinaison est populaire parce qu'à travers elle, tous ces facteurs deviennent plus aisément appréciables, récupérables par la multitude. Le design sexy tend à être inclusif plutôt qu'exclusif.

Nous avons donc ici un ensemble de créations extrêmement riche et varié. Les designers abordent chaque projet de manière délibérée, le contenu sexuel rendant le design plus accessible, tandis que le design favorise une approche de la sexualité plus imaginative ou plus réfléchie. Sexe et design ont la faculté de s'enrichir mutuellement.

Waar zijn we bang voor?

Seks interesseert iedereen, want iedereen doet het. Het koningshuis, politici, godsdienstige dignitarissen, kunstenaars, buren, collega's, je kinderen, je ouders en, ja, zelfs je ex. We vinden seks niet onschuldig, waarom zouden we ook? Als je geen seks hebt, wil je seks en hoe dan ook, je fantaseert er over, stelt vragen en houdt er een duidelijke mening op na. Designers maken een vergelijkbaar proces door in hun werk.Seks en design vormen een geslaagde combinatie. De luchtige seksconnotaties verlevendigen het design en verlossen het van een vaak elitaire bijsmaak. Rijk of arm, waar je ook vandaan komt, je hebt seks. Je ervaart het in levende lijve en je mening erover lijkt dan ook volkomen gerechtvaardigd. Iedereen begrijpt seks in design, of seksueel design, hoe geabstraheerd ook. Abstraheren: een gedetailleerde kijk op een concreet, in dit geval seksueel, idee. Iedereen is in staat obscene gedachten te vormen, zoals een gedetailleerde kijk op een seksueel idee vaak genoemd wordt.

Dit boek gaat over goede obscene ideeën: seks en design arm in arm; een overwinning op de vulgaire, borstvormige kurkentrekker of de eeuwige penisnoedels. Design en seks zijn beiden doordrongen van emotionele, sociaalculturele en visuele factoren. Hun combinatie is zo populair omdat al deze factoren plots ongedwongen overkomen en voor de grote massa gerecupereerd worden. Zolang we niet naar het prijskaartje kijken, is seksueel design eerder inclusief dan exclusief.

We stellen hier een buitengewoon rijke en gevarieerde collectie tentoon. De designers behandelden elk project met zorg en aandacht. De seksuele inhoud zorgt voor tastbaarheid en het design moedigt aan seks met fantasie en introspectie te benaderen. Seks en design kunnen elkaar alleen maar verrijken.

Cotton & Wool

Whippy, Voyeur, Love Honour Obey

Knowing when to get out is just as important as knowing when to get in, and True Love Always creator Jackie Beeke realized that during the second year of her Fine Arts degree. Her working experiences in the fashion and music industries*, and the artist contacts she made along the way finally gelled into the creation of True Love Always: sexy sheets that will send a crystal clear (if slightly intimidating) message to your next, or current bed buddy.

Savoir se retirer est aussi important que trouver de savoir entrer, et Jackie Beeke, créatrice de True Love Always, s'en est rendu compte lors de sa deuxième année d'études aux beaux-arts. Ses expériences professionnelles dans le monde de la mode et de la musique* ainsi que les contacts qu'elle s'est faits en chemin se sont concrétisés en donnant naissance à True Love Always, des draps sexy transmettant un message clair comme de l'eau de roche (limite intimidant) à quiconque partage, ou partagera, votre lit.

Op het juiste moment stoppen is net zo belangrijk als op het juiste moment beginnen. Dat besefte designer Jackie Beeke van True Love Always tijdens haar tweede jaar Kunstacademie. Haar werkervaring in de mode- en muziekindustrie* en haar contacten met artiesten kregen uiteindelijk vorm in True Love Always: sexy lakens met een kristalheldere (en soms enigszins intimiderende) boodschap voor je huidige of toekomstige bedgenoot.

*Including styling for England's only playboy photographer, and renowned perfectionist, Byron Newman.
*Dont le stylisme pour le seul photographe Anglais pour Playboy, et perfectionniste réputé, Byron Newman.
*Ze werkte zelfs voor Byron Newman, de enige playboyfotograaf van Engeland en befaamd om zijn perfectionisme.

Designer: True Love Always **Year:** 2005, 2006
Webmail: www.truelovealways.co.uk **Photo:** www.bartolomy.com

Make love not war

Blanket hogging has long been a favourite way to illustrate the corrosion of basic human decency in coupledom. As the ladies behind Miss Geschick and Lady Lapsus so aptly put it, "There is no room for aggression as long as one is properly equipped". An ironic comment about armed negotiation and "overly harmonious" relationships, these bed sheets "deal with those faux pas or delicate themes of the everyday life which we don't want to eliminate, but rather put in a positive context."

Le thème de la monopolisation de la couette est souvent utilisé pour illustrer la corrosion des rapports humains dans le couple. Comme le disent de façon fort appropriée les dames de Miss Geschick & Lady Lapsus, « Il n'y a pas de place pour l'agression tant que l'on est correctement équipé ». Commentaire ironique autant sur la négociation armée que les relations « trop harmonieuses », ces draps de lit « traitent la question de ces faux-pas ou thèmes délicats de la vie quotidienne qu'elles ne souhaitent pas éradiquer, mais replacer dans un contexte positif ».

Gekibbel over het laken is altijd al een populaire illustratie geweest van de afname van het menselijk fatsoen binnen relaties. Zoals de dames achter Miss Geschick en Lady Lapsus het zo mooi zeggen, "er is geen plaats voor agressie, zolang men maar het juiste gerei heeft". Als een ironisch commentaar op gewapende onderhandelingen en "al te harmonieuze" relaties, hebben deze lakens als Leitmotiv "die alledaagse vergissingen of delicate thema's die we niet willen elimineren, maar eerder in een positieve context plaatsen".

Designer: Miss Geschick & Lady Lapsus **Year:** 2006
Webmail: www.missgeschickladylapsus.de **Photo:** Nathalie Mohadjer, Laurentius Schmeier, Alexander Lembke

Masturbation cloths

Hansson founded Houseproud in 2005 after she discovered embroidery in Venice. She works with objects that are part of our everyday lives, "innocent" objects, or ones we are indifferent to. She decorates them in a traditional way, but the motifs come from a completely different world. "The masturbation cloth is an invented object- I think? A function that we all can imagine but maybe was never given a name and design. There are six masturbation cloths, one for every day, except for Sundays that are masturbation-free."

Hansson a fondé Houseproud en 2005 après avoir découvert la broderie à Venise. Ses travaux s'appliquent à des objets du quotidien, qu'ils soient « innocents », ou qu'ils nous laissent indifférents. Elle les décore en employant des procédés traditionnels, mais ses motifs proviennent d'un tout autre univers. « Le drap de masturbation est une de mes inventions – du moins je le crois. Il possède une fonction que chacun connaît, mais pour laquelle personne n'a encore créé d'objet avec un nom bien précis. Il existe six draps de masturbation, un pour chaque jour de la semaine, à l'exception des Dimanches qui sont sans masturbation ».

Hansson stichtte Houseproud in 2005, na haar ontdekking van de borduurkunst in Venetië. Ze werkt met voorwerpen uit het dagelijks leven, die "onschuldig" zijn of waar we onverschillig tegenover staan. Ze versiert ze op traditionele wijze, maar met motieven uit een totaal verschillende wereld. "Het masturbatiedoekje" is een verzonnen voorwerp, denk ik. Een makkelijk in te beelden functie, maar tot nu toe misschien zonder naam en design. Er zijn zes masturbatiedoekjes, één voor elke dag, behalve zondag, want die is masturbatievrij."

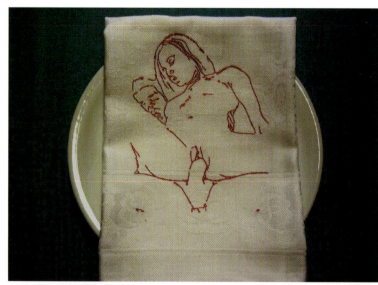

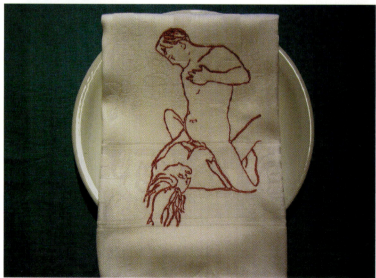

Designer: Houseproud **Year:** 2005
Webmail: www.houseproud.se **Photo:** Hansson

Oven mitts

Sometimes, Hansson adds a proverb or a saying to her embroidered objects in order to underline the metaphors in her work even further. Embroidery typified the "respectable" woman's pastime from the 17th to the 19th century. One of the few activities common to women of all classes, it was meant to keep them busy while men were taking care of important business. These oven mitts' multi-layered, cheeky innuendoes refer to women's role in society in past and present times.

Il arrive parfois que Hansson ajoute un proverbe ou un dicton à ses objets brodés pour souligner les métaphores sous-jacentes à ses travaux. La broderie était considérée comme le passe-temps respectable par excellence pour les femmes du XVIIe au XIXe siècle. L'une des rares activités communes à toutes les classes sociales, elle était destinée à les occuper pendant que leurs époux traitaient des affaires sérieuses. Sur ces gants de cuisine à multiples niveaux de lecture, les sous-entendus insolents évoquent leur rôle dans la société d'hier et d'aujourd'hui.

Soms voegt Hansson een gezegde of spreekwoord toe aan haar geborduurde voorwerpen, om de metaforen in haar werk extra te onderlijnen. Borduren was het typische "fatsoenlijk" vrouwelijk tijdverdrijf van de 17de tot de 19de eeuw. Het was één van de weinige activiteiten die vrouwen van alle standen bezig hield, terwijl de mannen de belangrijke zaken opknapten. De dubbelzinnige, brutale insinuaties op deze ovenwanten verwijzen naar de maatschappelijke rol van vrouwen, nu en vroeger.

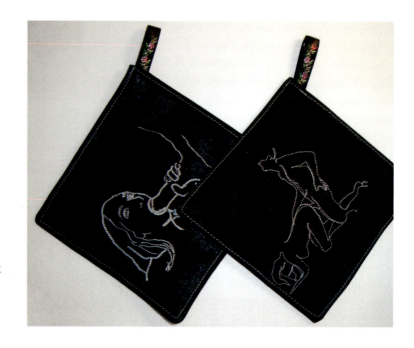

Designer: Houseproud **Year:** 2005
Webmail: www.houseproud.se **Photo:** Hansson

Towel Buddy

This beach towel by La tête au cube* is big enough for two, soft, and hand-embroidered. It was thought-up as an "anti-loneliness" device, however, it's also perfect as a "don't even bother" message to beach prowlers.

Ce drap de plage créé par La tête au cube* est assez grand pour deux personnes, doux au toucher et brodé à la main. Prévu à l'origine comme un accessoire « anti-solitude », il peut également signifier aux dragueurs des plages que ce n'est même pas la peine d'y penser.

Dit strandlaken van La tête au cube* is groot genoeg voor twee, zacht en handgeborduurd. Het is bedoeld als "anti-eenzaamheid"-middel, maar kan ook als "doe geen moeite"-boodschap voor strandloerders functioneren.

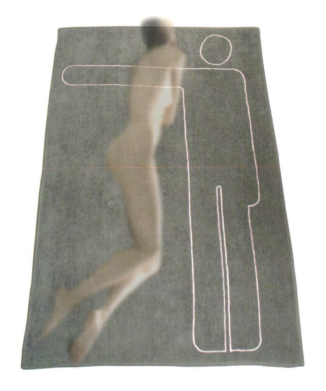

*Founded in 2005, La tête au cube develops new products created from a marketing perspective to fill little voids in design and concept. With no claim to revolutionizing the genre, they call their products "gentiment décalés", or "sweetly twisted".

* Agence créée en 2005, La tête au cube développe de nouveaux produits basés sur une approche marketing visant à combler des lacunes dans les domaines du concept et du design originaux. Sans prétendre révolutionner le genre, elle qualifie ses produits de « gentiment décalés ».

*Opgericht in 2005. Ontwikkelt nieuwe producten vanuit een marketingperspectief, om kleine leegtes in design en concept op te vullen. Ze noemen hun producten "gentiment décalés" of "een beetje getikt", zonder zich daarom revolutionair te noemen.

Designer: La tête au cube **Year:** 2005
Webmail: www.lateteaucube.com **Photo:** La tête au cube

Eat me out, girl on girl, Smut

We have tried, and tried, to pry information out of Sascha Quiambao about Smut, how it came into existence, who his hot friends are, who takes his steamy, porn-set-on-a-night-off pictures, etc., to no avail. When we asked for places, dates, something upon which to embroider, he answered, "Yes, I would rather that (we embroider)". We don't like embroidering (it's so 17th century), so plainly: Smut's semi-abstract sex motifs are hot.

Nous avons tenté, et re-tenté à plusieurs reprises d'extirper de Sascha Quiambao des informations sur sa compagnie, sur sa création, sur ses belles fréquentations, sur les auteurs de ses photos torrides style tournage-porno-au-repos – en vain. Nous lui avons demandé des lieux, des dates, des faits sur lesquels nous pourrions broder. Il nous a répondu : « Oui, je préférerais qu'on s'en tienne à ça (la broderie) ». Seulement, nous, on n'aime pas la broderie – ça fait très XVIIe siècle. Alors on se bornera à dire : les motifs sexuels semi abstraits de Smut sont chauds.

We hebben vruchteloos geprobeerd informatie los te peuteren uit Sascha Quiambao over Smut: hoe het begon, wie zijn geile vrienden zijn, wie de hete, porno-ploeg-op-vrije-avond-foto's maakt, enz. Toen we naar plaatsen en datums vroegen of iets anders om op verder te borduren, antwoordde hij, "Ja, doe dat maar (borduren)." Wij borduren niet graag (te 17de-eeuws), dus zonder omhalen: De semi-abstracte seksmotieven van Smut zijn geil.

Designer: Smut
Webmail: www.mysmut.eu.com **Photo:** Smut

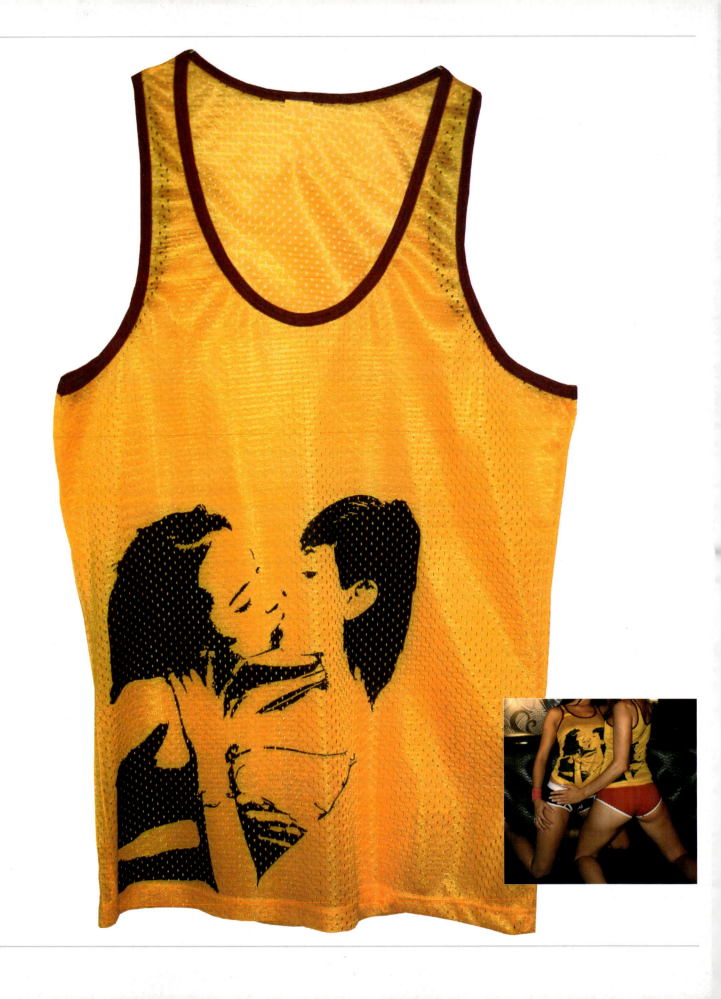

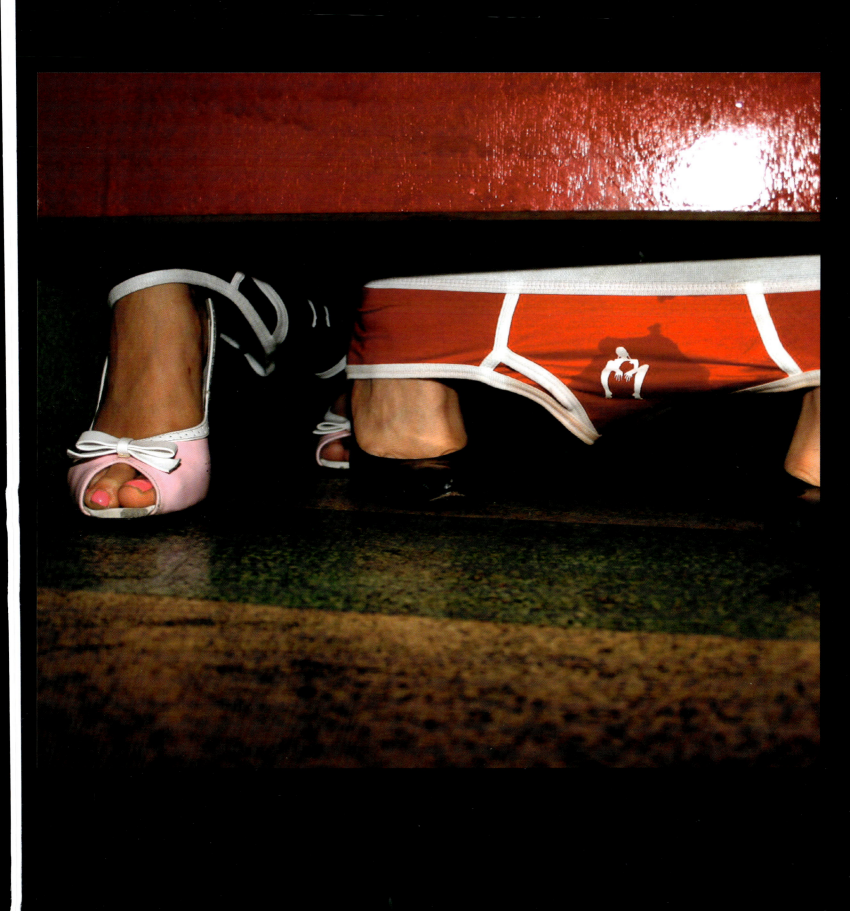

The Penis,
Fetal Underwear

This is one of Ninna Thorarinsdottir's solo projects. Confronting the fact that we adorn the outside of our bodies while finding our insides repulsive, Thorarinsdottir fools us into realizing it really shouldn't be so. When we first look at her pieces, we might be distracted by the pretty, outdated patterns, or our attention might immediately be drawn to the contrasting, tufted body elements. The Penis and The Foetal Underwear are paradoxically blatant and intimate reminders that what is found under our outside layer may be beautiful.

Ceci est l'un des projets solo de Ninna Thorarinsdottir. Partant du constat que nous décorons l'extérieur de notre corps tout en trouvant sa face interne répugnante, Thorarinsdottir nous trompe pour nous faire prendre conscience que les choses ne devraient pas fonctionner de cette manière. Certains seront attirés par les beaux motifs désuets au premier coup d'oeil, tandis que d'autres se focaliseront instantanément sur les contrastes des éléments corporels broussailleux. Le Penis et le Foetal Underwear nous rappellent d'une manière à la fois flagrante et intime que notre enveloppe externe recèle parfois une grande beauté intérieure.

Dit is één van Ninna Thorarinsdottir's soloprojecten. Thorarinsdottir maakt ons wijs dat het niet goed is dat we de buitenkant van ons lichaam versieren, maar de binnenkant walgelijk vinden. Op het eerste zicht kunnen haar werkstukken ons afleiden door hun mooie, ouderwetse motieven, maar ze kunnen ons ook onmiddellijk confronteren met de harige lichaamsdelen. The Penis en The Foetal Underwear zijn paradoxaal brutaal en herinneren er ons vertrouwelijk aan dat wat achter de buitenkant zit ook mooi kan zijn.

Designer: Fiska **Year:** 2005
Webmail: www.fiska.co.uk **Photo:** Ninna Thorarinsdottir

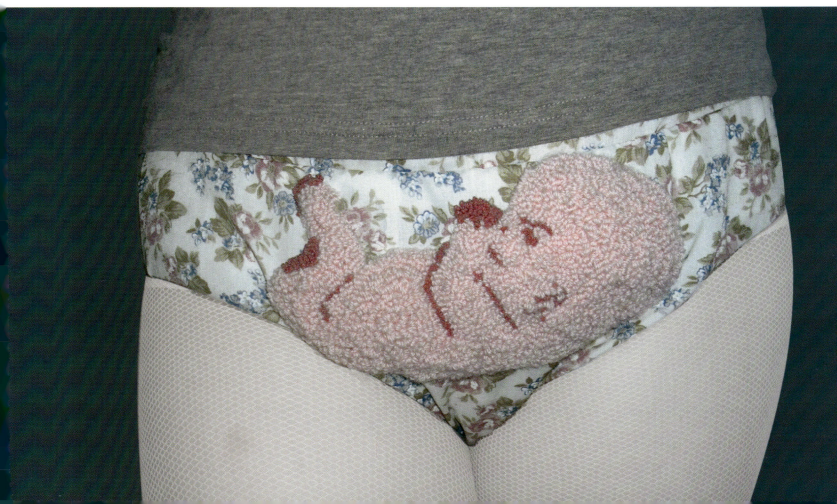

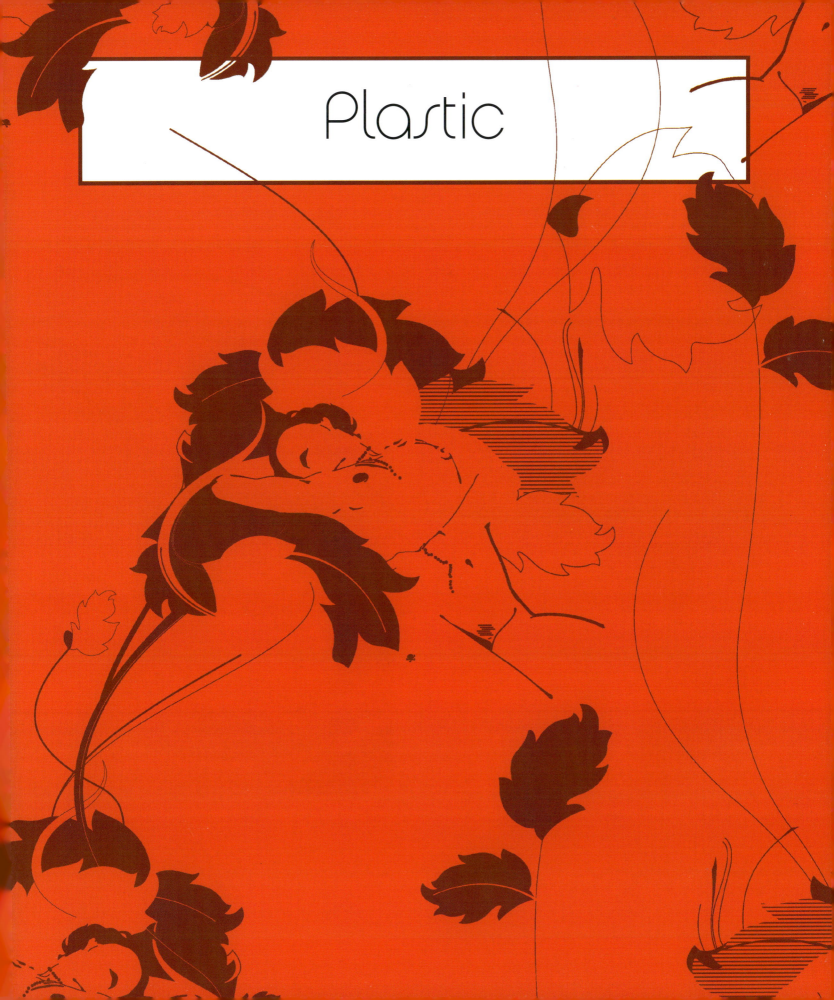

Plastic

Kundalini Mandala
Wall Lamp

Karim Rashid is a very prolific, very well known designer, and one of the few who outright smiles on his official portraits. Half Egyptian, half English, he now lives and works in New York City. His playful outlook has allowed him to engage in every imaginable creative domain, the project pages on his website run like CNN, constantly updated. The term "mandala", which the lamp is named after, has become a generic term for any geometric pattern representing the cosmos, metaphysically or symbolically, ergo, it is suggestive of the vagina.

Karim Rashid est un designer extrêmement prolifique et très connu, il est aussi l'un des rares à sourire franchement sur ses portraits officiels. Anglo-Égyptien, il vit et exerce actuellement à New York. Son esprit enjoué lui a permis de s'embarquer dans tous les domaines créatifs possibles et imaginables. Sur son site web, les pages de présentation de projets défilent comme celles d'un journal télévisé constamment remises à jour. Le terme « mandala » est devenu générique pour désigner tout motif géométrique qui représente le cosmos, métaphysiquement ou symboliquement. On y retrouve donc la suggestion du vagin.

Karim Rashid is een zeer productief en bekend designer en één van de weinigen die van harte lacht op officiële portretten. Hij is van Egyptische en Engelse afkomst, maar woont en werkt in New York. Zijn speelse uiterlijk verschaft hem toegang tot elk denkbaar creatief domein en de projecten op zijn website worden even vaak ge-update als die van de CNN. De term "mandala" staat voor gelijk welk geometrische motief dat de kosmos voorstelt, metafysisch of symbolisch, en suggereert zo ook de vagina.

Designer: Karim Rashid **Year:** 2006
Webmail: www.karimrashid.com **Photo:** Karim Rashid Inc.

Mr. P

Mr. P is a little character, a man of humour and pathos, whose penis used to be attached to a key ring, and now exists as a lamp switch (and god only knows how many more incarnations are planned for him in the future). His caption reads: "No wonder Mr. P is wearing a lampshade; wouldn't you if everyone kept flicking your titchy whangdoodle in order to turn on the light bulb in your head?". We couldn't have put it better, especially the "titchy whangdoodle" part.

Mr. P est un petit personnage, un homme à la fois amusant et pathétique, dont le pénis était autrefois attaché à un porte-clés et qui se présente aujourd'hui sous la forme d'un interrupteur de lampe (dieu seul sait combien de déclinaisons l'avenir lui réserve). Il porte l'inscription suivante : « Pas étonnant que Mr. P soit coiffé d'un abat-jour. Vous en feriez autant si l'on n'arrêtait pas de tripoter votre minuscule machinchose pour allumer l'ampoule située dans votre tête ». On ne peut mieux dire.

Mr. P is een hele persoonlijkheid, een man vol humor en pathos, met een penis die eerst als sleutelhanger diende en nu ook een schakelaar is (en god weet welke incarnaties hem nog te wachten staan). Het onderschrift luidt als volgt: "Geen wonder dat Mr. P een lampenkap op heeft; hoe zou je zelf zijn als iedereen voortdurend aan je piemeltje zat om de lamp in je hoofd aan te knippen?" We hadden het zelf niet beter kunnen stellen, vooral wat dat piemeltje betreft.

Designer: Zeon Ltd. **Year:** 2006
Webmail: www.firebox.com **Photo:** www.firebox.com

Leonardo

To paraphrase its creators, who speak of it so well: "Leonardo came from our desire to make a simple and beautiful object about intimacy, love and desire. The objects fossilize a moment of intimacy, Leonardo testifies of a story: we can still perceive the movements and the feelings in the immobility. And so form doesn't follow function, it follows the feelings. The object does not establish an innovation on a functional level, it emits an alternative message to the functionalist intention."

Laissons aux deux créateurs le soin de nous expliquer leur invention puisqu'ils en parlent si bien : « Leonardo est né de notre volonté de créer un objet simple et beau sur l'intimité, l'amour et le désir. Les objets fossilisent un moment d'intimité, Leonardo témoigne d'une histoire : on peut encore percevoir le mouvement et les sentiments dans l'immobilité. Ainsi, la forme ne suit pas la fonction, elle suit les émotions. L'objet n'établit pas une innovation à un niveau fonctionnel, il émet un message alternatif au propos fonctionnaliste ».

Om het te zeggen met de woorden van de trotse ontwerpers: "Met Leonardo wilden we een eenvoudig en mooi voorwerp maken gebaseerd op intimiteit, liefde en verlangen. Voorwerpen kunnen een intiem moment vastleggen. Leonardo is getuige van een verhaal: in zijn onbeweeglijkheid bespeuren we gebaren en gevoelens. Vorm heeft hier niets met functie te maken, maar wel met emoties. Het voorwerp is geen vernieuwing op functioneel vlak, maar wil eerder een alternatief voor het functionalisme zijn."

Designer: Bertrand Clerc & Olivier Gregoire **Year:** 2006
Photo: Bertrand Clerc & Olivier Gregoire

The Aphrodite Project platforms

Named after Aphrodite*, whose priestesses performed acts of prostitution as a sacred religious ritual (not much like today) and a social service (much like today). This smart shoe design appropriates the platform's shape to house a tracking GPS system that relays the wearer's location to public emergency services or to sex worker's rights groups (depending on the local legal status of prostitution) and an alarm system to repel attackers.

Ces chaussures reprennent le nom d'Aphrodite*, dont les prêtresses pratiquaient des actes de prostitution en tant que rituels religieux sacrés (plus vraiment d'actualité) et comme service rendu à la société (complètement d'actualité). Ce design astucieux utilise la semelle compensée pour abriter un système de localisation par GPS relayant la position de la porteuse soit aux services de secours publics, soit aux groupes de défense des droits des travailleuses du sexe, dépendant du statut légal de la prostitution à cet endroit. La semelle possède aussi un système d'alarme pour repousser les agresseurs.

Deze knappe schoen is naar Afrodite* genoemd, wiens priesteressen zich prostitueerden in een heilig, godsdienstig ritueel (niet zoals nu) en als een sociale dienst (zoals nu). De plateauvorm verbergt een alarmsysteem tegen mogelijke aanvallers, evenals een GPS waarmee de drager door de officiële hulpdiensten kan opgespoord worden, of, afhankelijk van de lokale wetgeving over prostitutie, door de vereniging voor de rechten van de seksarbeider.

*Ancient Greek goddess of fertility, raw sexuality, and/or love, depending on who your sources are.
*Déesse grecque de la fertilité, de la sexualité à l'état brut et/ou de l'amour, selon qui vous consultez.
*Oude Griekse godin van de vruchtbaarheid, de seks en/of de liefde, afhankelijk van de informatiebron.

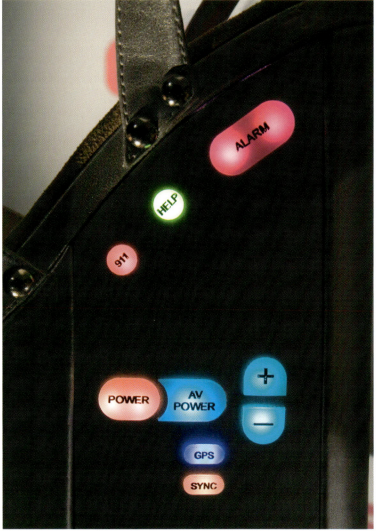

Designer: Norene Leddy **Year:** 2006
Webmail: www.theaphroditeproject.tv **Photo:** Elizabeth McCrocklin, Jesper Norgaard, Giselle Leal, Noreen Leddy

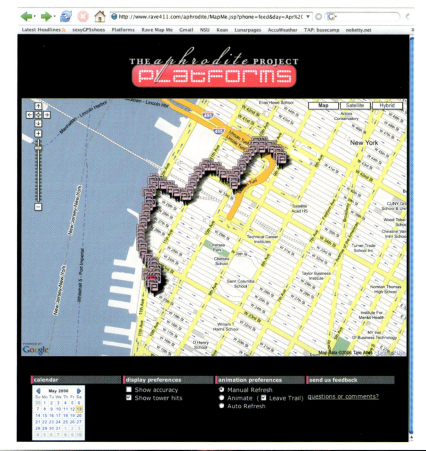

I rub my Duckie Paris

Many designers love to convert childhood items, otherwise known as deeply rooted signifiers of safety and innocence, into vibrating, orgasm-inducing companions. These vibrators could be dubbed the comfort food of sex toys. A variation on the traditional yellow model, the Paris Duckie's association with bath-time emphasizes their relaxing, "rub the day off" appeal, and their removable boa offers an extra tickle option. The perspective of playing doll with your vibrator might even hold special appeal for some of you out there...

Nombreux sont les designers qui aiment à détourner nos objets d'enfants, symboles de sécurité et d'innocence, en objets vibrants et orgasmiques. Ceux-cis pourraient être qualifiés « d'aliments de compensation » des jouets sexuels. Le modèle Paris, variante du canard jaune traditionnellement associé à l'heure du bain, met l'accent sur le caractère relaxant de l'objet qui permet de se détendre après une dure journée de travail. Son boa amovible offre la possibilité de bénéficier de chatouilles supplémentaires. L'idée de jouer à la poupée avec vos vibromasseurs pourrait même être d'un attrait particulier pour certains d'entre vous...

Vele designers houden er van voorwerpen uit hun kindertijd, diep ingewortelde symbolen van veiligheid en onschuld, om te bouwen tot vibrerende en orgasme-uitlokkende gezellen. Deze vibrators zijn het lekkere tussendoortje onder de seksspeeltjes. De Duckie Paris, een variatie op het traditionele gele badeendje, verwijst naar het relaxerende vergeet-je-zorgen-moment van het bad. De afneembare boa zorgt voor een extra prikkelmogelijkheid. En misschien vinden sommigen het wel een verleidelijk idee nog eens met de poppen te spelen, vibrator bij de hand...

Designer: Big Teaze Toys **Year:** 2006
Webmail: www.bigteazetoys.com **Photo:** Big Teaze Toys

Copulator stool

Agustin Otegui figured that "if sex sells, why not simply apply the principle in an explicit way and see if it works". The term "copulator" is part of the industrial design jargon, it refers to products that function according to a male/female assembly*. In this project, each stool plays a double role, giving and receiving-notwithstanding the endless hours of fun Mr. Otegui's illustrations will inspire to more than one bored, or adventurous, young man.

Agustin Otegui s'est dit : « Si le sexe fait vendre, pourquoi ne pas simplement appliquer ce principe d'une façon explicite et voir si ça marche »? Le terme « copulateur » désigne des produits qui fonctionnent par accouplement mâle-femelle* en jargon de design industriel. Dans ce projet, chaque tabouret joue un double rôle – donnant et recevant –. Sans compter les heures de jeu que les illustrations d'Otegui auront inspirées à plus d'un jeune homme d'humeur aventureuse, ou avec trop de temps libre sur les bras.

Agustin Otegui bedacht dat "als seks verkoopt, waarom het principe dan niet expliciet toepassen en zien of het werkt?" "Copulator" is een term uit het industrieel designjargon en verwijst naar producten met een mannelijk en vrouwelijk deel die in elkaar gepast worden*. In dit project speelt elk krukje de dubbele rol van geven en nemen, wat niet wegneemt dat Mr. Otegui hiermee eindeloze uren pret bezorgt aan talloze verveelde of avontuurlijke jonge mannen.

*The most obvious example of that principle would be the plug and socket.
*Exemple classique, la prise de courant.
*Het duidelijkste voorbeeld van dat principe is de stekker en het stopcontact.

Designer: Agustin Otegui **Year:** 2005
Webmail: www.agustin-otegui.com **Photo:** Agustin Otegui

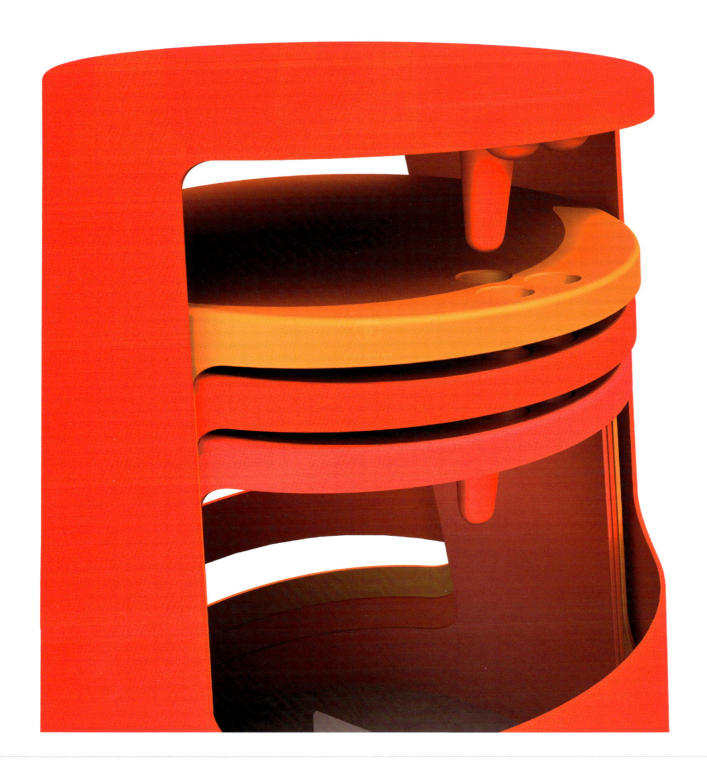

Sexy Beast line

It is a stretch of the imagination for most people to absorb the fact that a dog would care to be covered in "shimmering plant-based powders" or "lightweight laminating mist", but of course, these products are really addressed to humans. They are made of vegan ingredients, and "will make passing dogs go weak in the knees". Dogs don't go weak in the knees, they hump, but Karim Rashid's playful and clean design, combined with modern-day emotional alienation and anthropomorphic tendencies, will certainly appeal to the world Leaders of the Quest for glossiness.

Concevoir qu'un chien puisse en avoir quelque chose à faire d'être nappé de « poudres chatoyantes à base de plantes » ou bien d'une « brume lamineuse ultra-légère » requiert un gros effort d'imagination pour la majorité d'entre nous, mais évidemment, ces produits s'adressent plutôt aux humains. À base d'ingrédients végétaliens, ils sont sensés « faire craquer les autres chiens qui passent ». Les chiens ne « craquent » pas, ils copulent, mais les créations joueuses et épurées et Karim Rashid, conjuguées au sentiment d'aliénation émotionnelle et aux tendances anthropomorphes d'aujourd'hui, trouveront certainement un écho parmi nos Leaders dans la Quête du Lisse.

Het gaat de verbeelding van de meesten te boven dat een hond zich wel eens in "glinsterende plantaardige poeders" wil hullen, of in "laagjes lichtgewichtnevel", maar deze producten zijn dan ook in wezen voor mensen gemaakt. De ingrediënten zijn vegetarisch en "honden zullen er op slag verliefd op worden". Honden worden niet verliefd, ze neuken, maar het speelse en cleane design van Karim Rashid, in combinatie met de moderne emotionele vervreemding en antropomorfe tendensen, zal zeker aanslaan bij 's werelds Leiders van de Glimmerqueeste.

Designer: Karim Rashid **Year:** 2006
Webmail: www.karimrashid.com **Photo:** Karim Rashid Inc.

Tickle popzzz

Courtesy of Big Teaze Toys, here is another vibrating version of a
well-loved childhood item. And it works with two cell batteries!
Which will forever evoke bygone times, a generation who
remembers Game & Watch Donkey Kong. The lollipop is particularly
evocative to adults, a symbol of oral fixation loaded with Lolita
associations... The "sweet" part is made of soft rubber, and the
design even includes storage space at the base of the stick for an
extra set of batteries. We can just imagine them as a popular
post-party giveaway.

Big Teaze Toys nous propose une version vibrante d'un autre grand
classique enfantin, celle-ci fonctionne même avec deux piles
boutons qui ne manqueront pas de rappeler le bon vieux temps à la
génération qui a connu Donkey Kong. Particulièrement évocatrice
pour les adultes, la sucette est un symbole de fixation orale
étroitement associé au fantasme de la Lolita. La partie boule est
faite de caoutchouc tendre, tandis que le bâtonnet a un espace de
rangement pour deux piles supplémentaires. On imagine que ça
pourrait faire un bon cadeau souvenir après une fête.

Met dank aan Big Teaze Toys, nog een vibrerende versie van een
geliefd voorwerp uit onze kindertijd. Werkt met twee
celknoopbatterijen! Een dierbare herinnering voor de generatie
van de eerste computerspelletjes. Voor volwassenen is een lolly
bijzonder suggestief, een symbool van orale fixatie vol Lolita-
associaties. Het "zoete" deel is van zacht rubber en in het handvat
is zelfs een opbergruimte voor extra batterijen voorzien. Een
perfect "postfuif-weggevertje", toch?

Designer: Big Teaze Toys **Year:** 2006
Webmail: www.bigteazetoys.com **Photo:** Big Teaze Toys

Plexibox

LuLúxpo is the contraction of two names, Lulú and Pollux. This couple covers a lot of ground: music, fashion, product and graphic design, art, party planning, mixing, community activating, parenting... Their approach may seem slightly "bubblegum", but a longer look reveals two committed professionals with a lot of ambition: their message and motivator, "Love is power", is pertinent and simple. This condom distributor illustrates their festive and "transparent" attitude towards love, sex, and responsibility.

LuLúxpo est la contraction des noms Lulú et Pollux, un couple dont les travaux englobent de nombreux domaines : musique, mode, design produit, graphisme, organisation d'évènements, DJ, animation communautaire, et ils sont parents... Si leur approche peut paraître quelque peu « bubblegum», un examen plus approfondi révèle deux professionnels consciencieux et pleins d'ambition, motivés par un message pertinent et simple : « l'amour est pouvoir». Leur distributeur de préservatifs illustre cette approche festive et « transparente » envers l'amour, le sexe et la responsabilité individuelle.

LuLúxpo is de samentrekking van twee namen, Lulú en Pollux. Dit koppel houdt zich met heel wat thema's bezig: muziek, mode, productdesign, grafisch design, kunst, feestplanning, mixen, gemeenschapswerk, ouderschap... Hun aanpak mag dan ietwat "bubblegum" aandoen, als je wat beter kijkt zie je twee toegewijde, ambitieuze professionelen: hun boodschap "Love is power" is raak en simpel. Deze condoomautomaat illustreert hun feestelijke en "transparante" houding tegenover liefde, seks en verantwoordelijkheid.

Designer: LuLúxpo **Year:** 2005
Webmail: www.luluxpo.com **Photo:** LuLúxpo

Luxit Unikorn

These luminous, modular and evocative clothes racks can be arranged in any way you please. For hooking, hanging, and lighting, they bring comfort when you come home to a dark hallway, drunk from a hard day's work or a crazy party. They also create a flattering, sexy light; its soft glow is perfect for the bathroom. Stepping out of a shower for two, you can tease your lover with an extra flash of light before covering yourself up with the towel that was hanging on it not a second ago.

Modulables et évocateurs, ces portemanteaux lumineux peuvent êtres disposés comme bon vous semble. Servant de crochet, de cintre et d'éclairage, ils apportent une touche de réconfort dans l'obscurité de votre entrée lorsque vous titubez d'ivresse après une dure journée de labeur ou une folle soirée. La lumière flatteuse sensuelle et douce qu'ils émettent s'adapte parfaitement à la salle de bains. Sortant d'une douche prise à deux, vous pourrez aguicher votre amant d'un flot de lumière avant d'envelopper votre corps nu dans la serviette qui y était suspendue il n'y a pas un instant.

Deze lichtgevende, modulaire en suggestieve kleerhangers kan je naar eigen believen rangschikken. Ze brengen een opwindend sprankelend lichtje in de donkere gang als je dronken thuiskomt van een harde werkdag of een waanzinnige fuif. Ze geven ook een zachte, flaterend sexy gloed die perfect in de badkamer past. Na een douche voor twee kan je je minnaar plagen met een extra lichtflits, alvorens je de handdoek om je heen slaat die er net nog ophing.

Designer: Karim Rashid **Year:** 2006
Webmail: www.karimrashid.com **Photo:** Karim Rashid Inc.

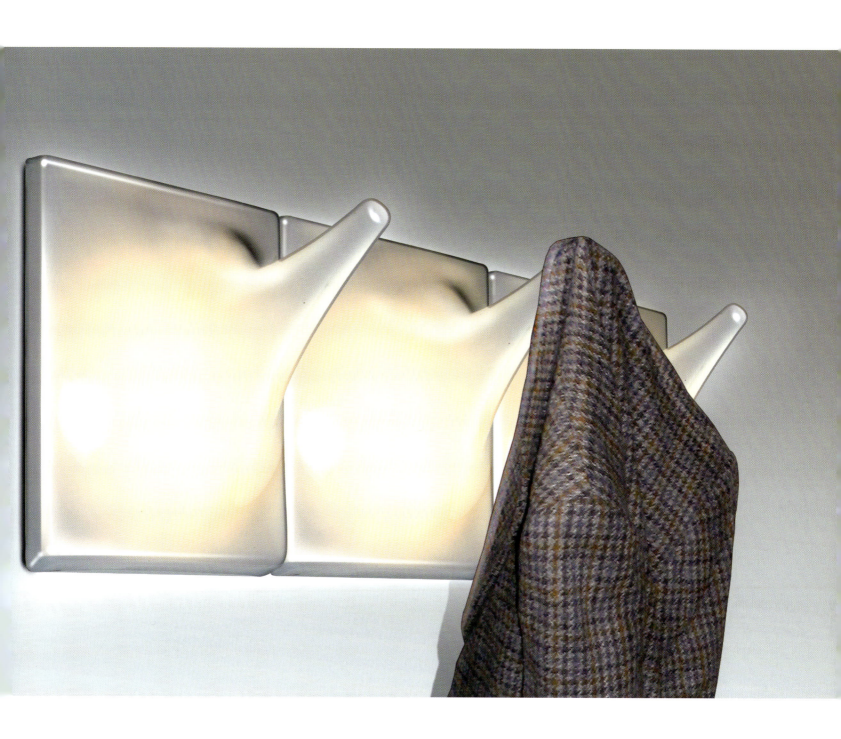

Buddies

Paul Derrez's "Buddies" pendants are made of Corian® plastic, and they hang from a woven silk string. They are almost dainty compared to his earlier work, looking a little like streamlined exotic flower buds. Designed as an exploration of form, colour, and new materials, they are hard, but retain body heat- sexy not just because of their function as a sex toy, but also because they attract the eye and invite to the touch. Quoting Derrez about his own work, "they seem to have the most appeal where one's own sexuality and the desired object coincide."

Suspendus à un collier de soie tissée, les pendentifs « Buddies » de Paul Derrez sont en plastique Corian®. Plus délicats que ses réalisations précédentes, ils évoquent des boutons de fleur exotique profilés. Fruits d'une exploration sur le thème de la forme, de la couleur et des nouveaux matériaux, ils sont durs au toucher, mais absorbent la chaleur du corps. Leur érotisme n'est pas simplement dû à leur fonction masturbatoire, ils invitent aussi le toucher et le regard. Pour reprendre les termes de Derrez, « le pouvoir d'attraction semble s'exercer le plus fortement lorsque la sexualité de la personne et l'objet désiré coïncident ».

Paul Derrez's "Buddies" hangertjes zijn gemaakt van Corian® en hangen aan een geweven zijden draad. Ze zijn bijna sierlijk vergeleken met zijn vroegere werk, en hebben wat weg van gestroomlijnde, exotische bloemknoppen. Ze zijn een zoektocht naar vorm, kleur en nieuwe materialen. Ze zijn hard en houden de lichaamswarmte vast. Sexy als seksspeeltje, maar ook omdat ze visueel aantrekkelijk zijn en vragen om aangeraakt te worden. We citeren Derrez: "ze zijn het aantrekkelijkst als je eigen seksualiteit en het begeerde object samenvallen."

Designer: Paul Derrez **Year:** 1999
Webmail: www.galerie-ra.nl **Photo:** Paul Derrez

1 set partout

A poetic take on the "copulator"* principle, La tête au cube's placemats penetrate each other. They are beautiful and make a lot of sense in pairs, but look clumsy without the other. Their form and function flow together, encouraging communication and attention. Psychologists and counsellors often advise couples or family members in an argument to establish physical contact with each other. Apparently, touching breaks down barriers, which allows for better communication.

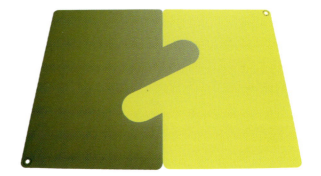

Application poétique du principe « copulateur »* le set de table de La tête au cube se compose de deux éléments qui s'interpénètrent. Beaux et chargés de signification lorsqu'ils sont en couple, ils ont l'air maladroits l'un sans l'autre. La communion entre leur forme et leur fonction incite la communication et l'attention. Les psychologues et les conseillers conjugaux recommandent souvent aux couples et aux familles en pleine dispute d'établir un contact physique. En effet, le toucher fait tomber les barrières et favorise la communication.

De onderleggers van La tête au cube penetreren elkaar en zijn zo een poëtische interpretatie van het "copulator"* principe. Samen zijn ze mooi en zinvol, maar in hun eentje zien ze er onhandig uit. Vorm en functie vloeien in elkaar over om communicatie en aandacht te stimuleren. Psychologen en consulenten raden ruziënde koppels of familieleden vaak aan fysiek contact te maken met elkaar. Elkaar aanraken slecht blijkbaar grenzen en bevordert de communicatie.

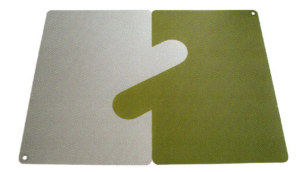

*The male/female assembly principle mentioned earlier.
*Principe d'accouplement mâle-femelle exposé précédemment.
*Het eerder vermelde in-elkaar-pas-principe.

Designer: La tête au cube **Year:** 2005
Webmail: www.lateteaucube.com **Photo:** La tête au cube

Valentine Néa

Valentine's day sells cards, flowers, chocolates and vibrators. You
   might as well get your bed-buddy a good one, and the special
   edition Black Pearl Valentine Néa is just that, especially if it's the
   first time you traipse that kind of ground together. Designed in
   collaboration with Jesper Kouthoofd (of ACNE* fame), the most
   neo-post-modern vibrator yet combines an innocent looking,
   archetypal heart tattoo motif with a slick Mac finish, and it will
   turn on any design blogosphere princess.

La Saint-Valentin vend des cartes de voeux, des fleurs, des chocolats
   et des vibromasseurs. Si c'est la première fois que vous explorez
   ce domaine avec votre partenaire, autant choisir un bon modèle.
   Le Black Pearl Valentine Néa, en édition limitée, est exactement ce
   qu'il vous faut. Conçu en partenariat avec Jesper Kouthoofd (du
   groupe ACNE*), c'est le plus néopostmoderne des vibromasseurs.
   Combinant un archétypal coeur tatoué à l'air innocent, et une
   finition soignée style Apple Mac, il ne manquera pas d'exciter
   toute princesse de la blogosphère design.

Op Valentijnsdag verkoopt men kaartjes, bloemen, bombons én
   vibrators. Je kan maar beter een goede kopen voor je bedgenoot,
   zoals de speciale editie Black Pearl Valentine Néa, en zeker als jullie
   je voor het eerst samen op dit terrein wagen. Dit toppunt van neo-
   post-moderne vibrators werd in samenwerking met Jesper
   Kouthoofd (bekend van ACNE*) ontworpen en combineert een
   onschuldige, archetypische harttatoeage met een strakke Mac-
   afwerking. Hier wordt elke design-blogprinses opgewonden van.

*ACNE, a Swedish design compound: digital, graphic, fashion, print...
*ACNE, un conglomérat de design suédois : numérique, graphisme, mode, print...
*ACNE, een Zweedse designgroep: digitaal, grafisch, mode, print...

Designer: Lelo & Jesper Kouthoofd **Year:** 2007
Webmail: www.lelo.com **Photo:** Katja Kristofersson

Form 6

Form 6 was about to be publicly launched when we asked Jimmyjane what was going to be so "revolutionary" about it. We were kindly asked to wait a few hours until it was put up on the website. When we checked back a couple of weeks later, Form 6 was already sold out. Somebody there is certainly doing his or her job right. Rechargeable, waterproof, Form 6 is very tech, but not in an "I download programs from the Net to jerk off to" way. It blends innovative dual motor vibrations and an Escher-like, continuous silicone surface for utmost intuitive versatility...

Form 6 était sur le point d'être mis sur le marché lorsque nous avons demandé à Jimmyjane ce qu'il allait avoir de si « révolutionnaire ». On nous a aimablement invités à patienter quelques heures avant sa mise en vente sur le site web. Lorsque nous sommes allés voir quelques semaines plus tard, Form 6 était déjà en rupture de stock, on peut donc en déduire qu'ils ont fait du bon boulot. Rechargeable et étanche, Form 6 est high-tech, sans donner dans le « je télécharge mes programmes masturbation sur internet ». Il combine un système novateur à deux moteurs et une surface en silicone continue, à la Escher, assurant ainsi polyvalence et utilisation des plus intuitives.

Form 6 stond op het punt om uit te komen toen we Jimmyjane vroegen wat er nu zo "revolutionair" aan was. We werden vriendelijk verzocht een paar uur te wachten tot het op de website stond. Toen we het een paar weken later bekeken, was Form 6 al uitverkocht. Blijkbaar doet er iemand daar zijn werk goed. Form 6 is oplaadbaar, waterdicht en erg "tech", maar niet in de zin van "ik download programma's om me bij af te rukken". Een harmonieuze mix van dubbele motorvibraties en een Escher-achtig, naadloos siliconen oppervlak voor uiterst intuïtieve wendbaarheid.

Designer: Jimmy Jane **Year:** 2007
Webmail: www.jimmyjane.com **Photo:** Jimmyjane

Paper

Porte-jarretelle, Smocking, Bottes, Cuissardes, Amour

After a successful career as an advertisement Art Director specialized in promoting cars and the like, Joël le Berre turned to the soft side and went to work for ultra-chic lingerie creator Chantal Thomass*. He decidedly engaged in her world of strong contrasts and refined details with the creation of these hosiery packs.

À l'issue d'une carrière bien remplie en tant que directeur artistique dans la promotion automobile et autres industries du genre, Joël le Berre s'est tourné vers le côté doux en allant travailler pour la créatrice de lingerie fine Chantal Thomass*. Le Berre s'est lancé dans le monde fort en contrastes et en raffinements de Thomass avec conviction, comme en témoigne ce nouveau packaging.

Na een succesvolle carrière als Art Director bij een publiciteitsfirma gespecialiseerd in de autoindustrie, bekeerde Joël le Berre zich tot het softere werk en begon hij te creëren voor de ultra chique lingerie-ontwerper Chantal Thomass*. Hij liet zich vastbesloten in met haar wereld van felle contrasten en verfijnde details om deze verpakkingen te ontwerpen.

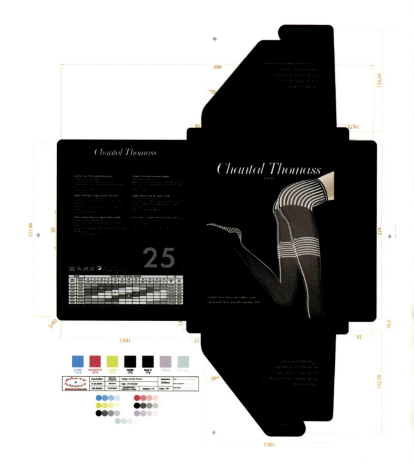

*Previous baiting experience includes precursory teasing campaign "Myriam enlève le haut, puis le bas", in which a woman promises to take her top, then her bottom off (she does so, but turns her back to us in the last image).
*Antécédents d'appâteur, il était l'initiateur de la célèbre campagne de teasing « Myriam enlève le haut, puis le bas », dans laquelle Myriam se dénude en effet, mais en nous tournant finalement le dos.
*Ervaring in de verleidingskunst deed hij op met de reclamecampagne "Myriam enlève le haut, puis le bas", waarin een vrouw belooft eerst haar top uit te trekken en daarna haar slipje (hetgeen ze doet, hoewel ze zich op het laatste moment omdraait).

Designer: Joël le Berre for Chantal Thomass **Year:** 2007
Photo: Joël le Berre, Chantal Thomass

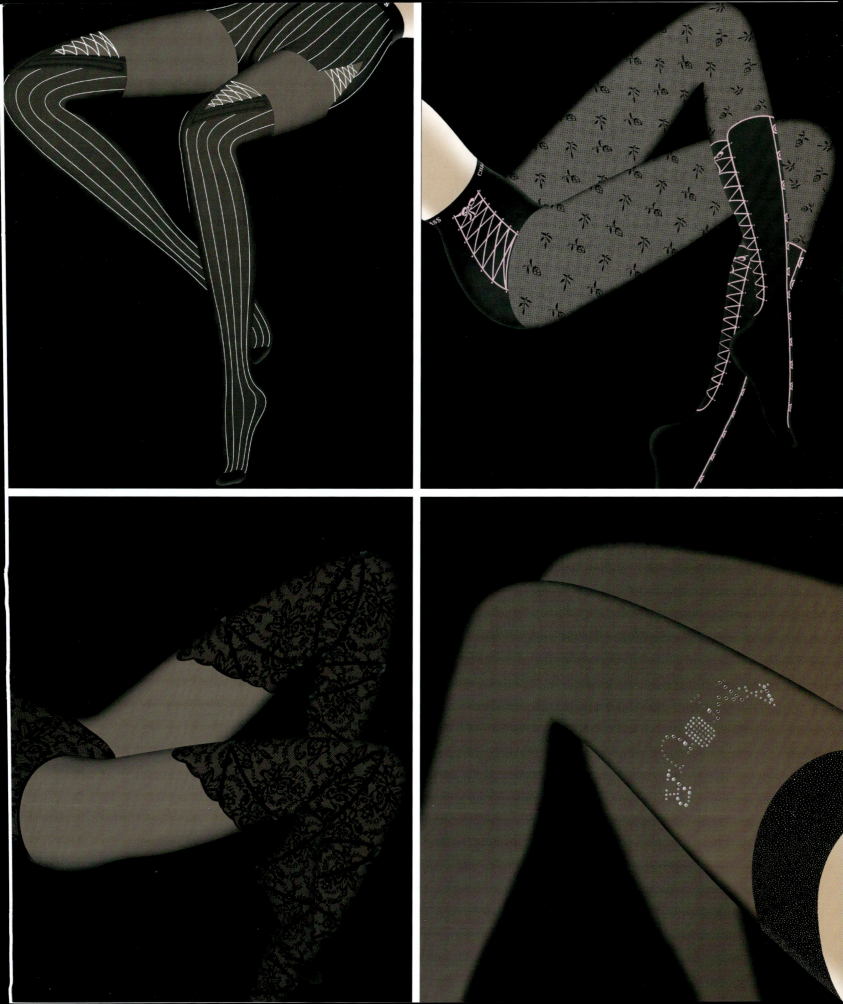

Wallpaper

DED Associates is behind Paper Voyeur. An independent and successful design studio which (rightly) holds on to privileges such as calling their website DedAss or their Resume section "blah blah blah", DED's oft-commissioned work is very diverse. Taking their maximal approach to wallpaper, the result is a mix of lush pattern, juicy colour, and varying finishes. Just erotic enough to be worth it, but with a touch of reserve that actually makes it a conceivable public option. Agent Provocateur recently snatched them up for their new store.

DED Associates sont les créateurs de Paper Voyeur. Un studio de design indépendant et s'accrochant (avec raison) à des privilèges tels que celui de se permettre d'appeler leur site web DedAss (« t'es mort ») et sa section CV « bla, bla, bla », DED travaille sur une grande variété de projets. Retranscrivant leur approche maximale au papier peint, le résultat associe motifs luxuriants et couleurs juteuses dans une variété de finitions. Suffisamment érotique pour en valoir la peine, ce papier fait cependant preuve d'une certaine réserve qui en fait un choix envisageable pour un lieu public. Agent Provocateur vient d'ailleurs de le retenir pour sa dernière boutique.

Achter Paper Voyeur zit DED Associates, een onafhankelijke en succesvolle designstudio die zich (terecht) het recht toeëigent om hun wesite DEDAss te noemen en hun CV "blah blah blah". Hun wijd geapprecieerde werk is zeer divers. Ze maken behangpapier dat een mix is van weelderige motieven, sappige kleuren en gevarieerde afwerking. Net erotisch genoeg om de moeite waard te zijn, maar subtiel genoeg voor gebruik in publieke ruimtes. Agent Provocateur heeft hen onlangs aan de haak geslagen voor zijn nieuwe winkel.

Designer: Paper Voyeur **Year:** 2006
Webmail: www.papervoyeur.com **Photo:** Paper Voyeur

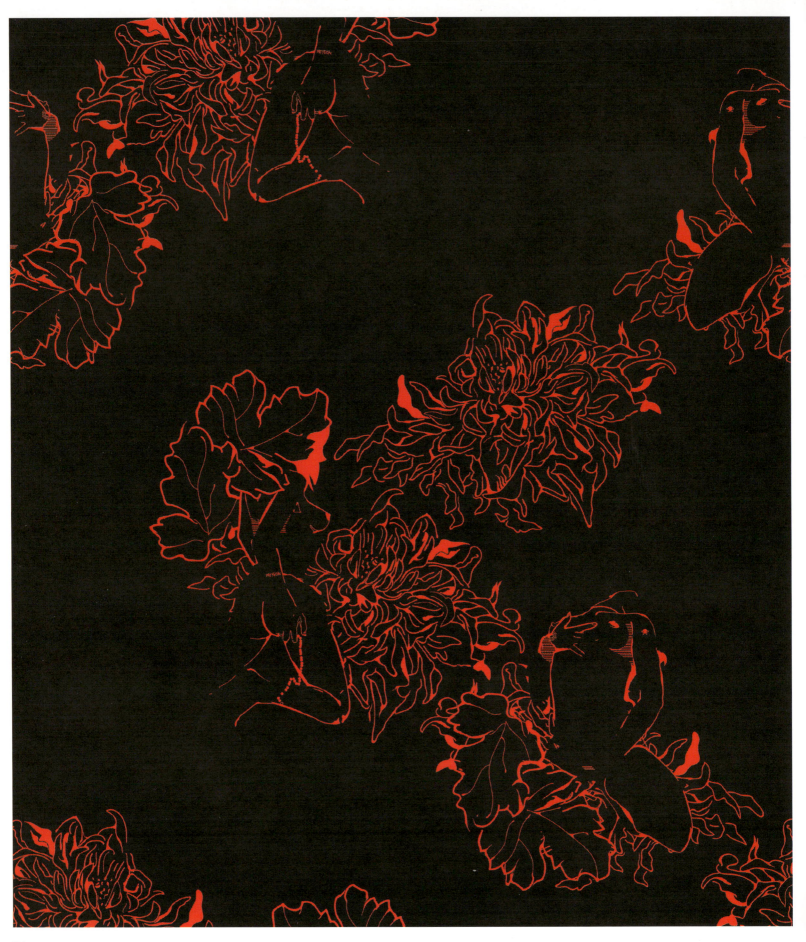

74

Dew, You've got porn

Mirko Ilič was born in Bosnia and moved to the US in 1986. He was an Art Director for the international edition of Time and The New York Times Op-Ed pages, and in 1995, he established Mirko Ilic Corp. These pieces were originally published in the Village Voice: "dew", from his ongoing personal series Sex & Lies, and "You've got Porn", which illustrated an article by the same name*. The article dealt with AOL, a self-proclaimed "family orientated company", as one of the biggest providers of porn in the world.

Né en Bosnie, Mirko Ilič s'est installé aux Etats-Unis en 1986. Ex-directeur artistique pour l'édition internationale de Time et les pages de chroniques du *New York Times*, il a fondé Mirko Ilic Corp en 1995. Ces illustrations furent publiées pour la première fois dans *Village Voice* : « Dew » fait partie de sa série personnelle intitulée « Sex & Lies » (« sexe et mensonges »), tandis que « You've got Porn » accompagnait un article du même nom* traitant d'AOL (« une entreprise à vocation familiale ») en tant que l'un des plus grands pourvoyeurs de pornographie au monde.

De in Bosnië geboren Mirko Ilič verhuisde in 1986 naar de VS. Hij werkte als Art Director voor de internationale editie van Time en de The New York Times Op-Ed pagina's. In 1995 stichtte hij Mirko Ilic Corp. Deze werken werden oorspronkelijk in de Village Voice uitgegeven: "Dew", uit zijn huidige persoonlijke reeks Sex & Lies en "You've got Porn"*, een illustratie bij een gelijknamig artikel. Het artikel ging over AOL, een naar eigen zeggen "familiegericht bedrijf" en één van de grootste pornoleveranciers ter wereld.

*A play on AOL's famous "You've got mail" catchphrase.
*Jeu de mot sur la célèbre phrase d'AOL « You've got mail » (« Vous avez un message »).
*Een woordspeling op AOL's beroemde "You've got mail"-cliché.

Designer: Mirko Ilič **Year:** 2004, 2003
Webmail: www.mirkoilic.com

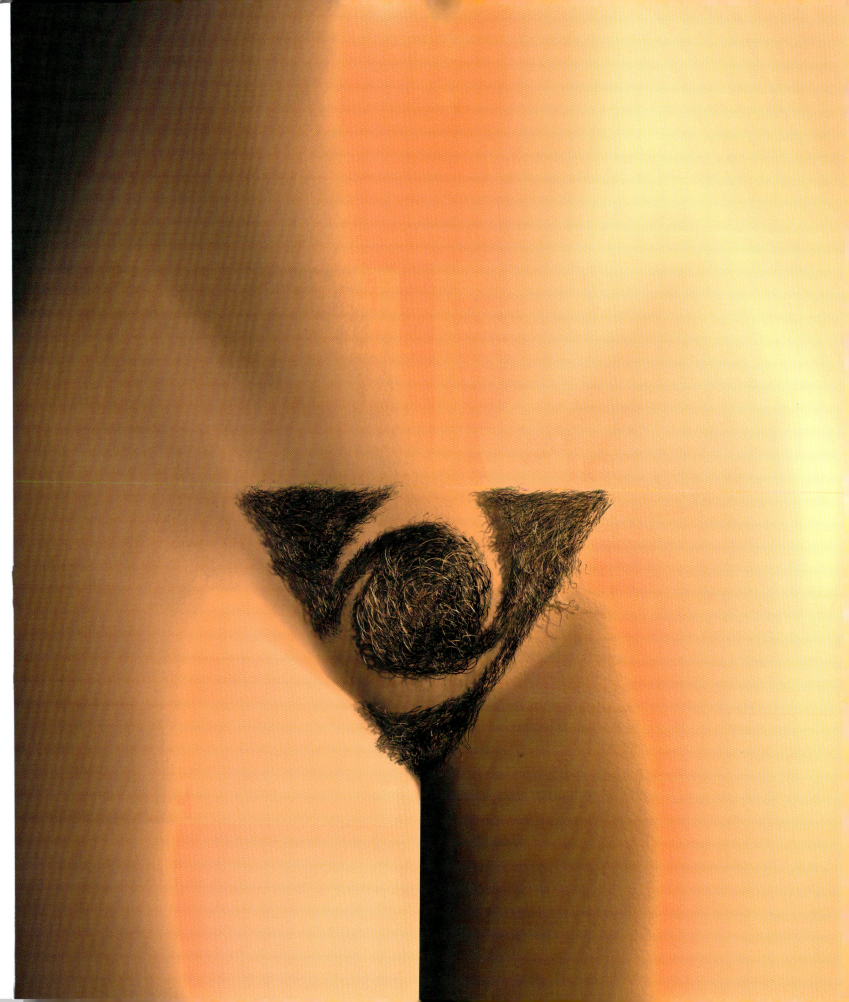

Sexy

Newtree combines the inherent benefits of chocolate* with natural extracts and a medley of flavours. Sexy is a mix of dark Belgian chocolate and ginger, and these two ingredient's aphrodisiac qualities are enhanced by guarana extract (a natural stimulant).

Newtree associe les bienfaits du chocolat* à des extraits naturels et un mélange de parfums. Sexy est le mariage du chocolat belge noir et du gingembre, deux ingrédients dont les qualités aphrodisiaques se voient renforcées par l'apport d'extrait de guarana, un stimulant naturel.

Newtree combineert de goede eigenschappen van chocolade* met natuurlijke extracten en een mengeling van aroma's. Sexy is een mix van zwarte Belgische chocolade en gember, twee afrodisiaca die nog eens versterkt worden door guarana-extract (een natuurlijk stimulerend middel).

*It is often said that chocolate has a similar chemical build-up to love; in fact, it is packed with dopamine (dopamine neurons are activated when an unexpected reward is presented. In nature, we learn to repeat behaviours that lead to unexpected rewards) and serotonin (produces a sensation similar to heroin).

*On dit souvent que la composition chimique du chocolat ressemble à celle de l'amour. C'est dû au fait qu'il contient de la dopamine (stimule les neurones lorsqu'une récompense inattendue se présente ; de façon naturelle, nous apprenons à réitérer les comportements susceptibles de produire des récompenses inattendues) et de la sérotonine (substance qui produit une sensation semblable à celle de l'héroïne).

*Men zegt vaak dat chocolade chemisch gezien op liefde lijkt. In werkelijkheid bevat het een hoop dopamine (de dopamineneuronen worden geprikkeld bij onverwachte beloningen. De natuur leert ons gedrag dat beloond wordt te herhalen) en serotonine (heeft een effect vergelijkbaar aan heroïne).

Designer: Newtree **Year:** 2005
Webmail: www.newtree.com **Photo:** Newtree

Wrapping Paper

Mr. Finkelstein has an interesting history as a designer and a political activist.* "I am gay. Gay people are always surrounded by images that reflect heterosexual life, like the pastoral reveries found in classic toile patterns. I liked the graphic quality of toile, but wanted one that related to the gay experience." Thus, the Dirty Linens Tom of Finland pattern. After enough requests for a woman's version came in, the Girl Power pattern was born.

M. Finkelstein à une histoire intéressante en tant que designer et activiste politique.* « Je suis gay. Les gays sont entourés en permanence d'images qui reflètent le mode de vie hétérosexuel, à l'instar des rêveries champêtres que l'on retrouve dans les motifs toile classiques. J'aimais la qualité graphique de la toile, mais j'en voulais une qui reflète l'expérience gay. » C'est ainsi qu'ont vu le jour les Dirty Linens à motif « Tom of Finland ». Suite à une forte demande pour une version féminine, Finkelstein a créé le motif Girl Power.

Mr. Finkelstein heeft een interessant verleden als designer en politiek activist.* "Ik ben gay. Gays zijn altijd omringd door beelden uit het heteroseksuele leven, zoals de pastorale mijmerij op het klassieke Toile de Jouy behang. De grafische kwaliteit van de Toile de Jouy bevalt me, maar ik wou iets gay-vriendelijkers." Vandaar het Dirty Linens Tom of Finland-motief. Toen er ook vraag kwam naar een vrouwelijke versie, ontstond het Girl Power-motief.

*He created the disquieting Silence=Death poster associated with AIDS activism in the mid-80s, for instance.
*C'est lui qui a dessiné, entre autres, la troublante affiche « Silence=Death », associée à l'activisme contre le SIDA au milieu des années 1980.
*Midden jaren 80 ontwierp hij bijvoorbeeld de verontrustende Silence=Death poster ivm het aids-activisme.

Designer: Dirty Linens **Year:** 2005, 2004
Webmail: www.groovyg.com **Photo:** Dirty Linens

Illustrations

Parra's illustrations are puzzling at first, then quickly become addictive, a bit like Enjoi ads or Frusciante records. Depending on who you ask, they are weird, or not weird enough, too niche-y or too vulgar, great, or plain ugly. Few illustrators find a completely personal voice, and even fewer manage to address sex and gender issues in a visually direct manner while delivering rich content. Whether you warm up to his aesthetic or not, you will find that his images are strong, yet open-ended. They combine emotional response, thoughtfulness, and humour.

Dans un premier temps, les illustrations de Parra laissent perplexe, mais on en devient rapidement accro, un peu comme les pubs d'Enjoi ou la musique de Frusciante. D'aucuns les considèrent trop étranges, d'autres pas assez, certains les trouvent trop averties, d'autres trop vulgaires, tantôt géniales ou carrément moches. Peu d'illustrateurs se forgent une voix totalement personnelle. Plus rares encore sont ceux qui traitent les questions de sexe d'une manière aussi directe au niveau visuel, tout en préservant une forte richesse de contenu. Que vous soyez sensible ou pas à son sens esthétique, vous verrez que ses images sont puissantes, tout en restant ouvertes. Elles conjuguent réaction émotionnelle, réflexion, et humour.

De illustraties van Parra zijn op het eerste zicht onthutsend, maar werken al gauw verslavend, een beetje zoals de reclame van Enjoi of de albums van Frusciante. De meningen zijn verdeeld: raar of niet raar genoeg, te elitistich of te vulgair, geweldig of ronduit lelijk. Weinig illustrators vinden een volledig eigen stem en nog minder slagen erin seks en geslachtskwesties met inhoud op een visueel directe manier te brengen. Of je nu warm loopt voor deze esthetica of niet, deze beelden moet je wel sterk vinden, hoewel ze ook vrijblijvend zijn. Ze combineren emotionele respons, bedachtzaamheid en humor.

Designer: Parra **Year:** 2006, 2007
Webmail: www.bigactive.com, www.rockwellclothing.com

Pornographic wallpaper

The term "Expatriate" is especially suited for those who found what they were looking for in Mexico City. The rest of the world seems to fade when you find yourself immersed in this seething sprawl of a city and its particular brand of logic*. Carlos Ranc was born in France and lives in D.F., where he creates wallpaper that is quite in keeping with this logic. The pornographic motifs are presented in a flower-patterned book, which both offsets and complements its content.

Le terme « expatrié » désigne à la perfection les personnes qui ont trouvé ce qu'elles recherchaient à Mexico. Une fois immergé dans cette mégapole bouillonnante et tentaculaire où règne une logique très particulière*, le reste du monde à tendance à s'estomper. Né en France, Carlos Ranc vit aujourd'hui à Mexico, où il crée des papiers peints correspondant bien à cette logique. Ses motifs pornographiques sont catalogués dans un livre à fleurs qui complémente et contrebalance son contenu.

De term "Expatriate" is bijzonder gepast voor zij die vonden wat ze zochten in Mexico City. De rest van de wereld vervaagt, zodra je onderduikt in deze bruisende stadschaos en zijn aparte logica*. Carlos Ranc is geboren in Frankrijk en woont in D.F., waar hij behangpapier ontwerpt dat die logica op de voet volgt. De pornografische motieven worden voorgesteld in een boek met bloemendessin, dat zijn inhoud zowel neutraliseert als aanvult.

*Witness it through the excellent work of another Ex-pat, Belgian artist Francis Alÿs.
*Soyez-en témoin au travers de l'excellent travail d'un autre expatrié, l'artiste Belge Francis Alÿs.
*Getuige hiervan is het excellente werk van een andere Expat, de Belgische kunstenaar Francis Alÿs.

Designer: Carlos Ranc **Year:** 2004
Webmail: carlosranc@gmail.com **Photo:** Carlos Ranc

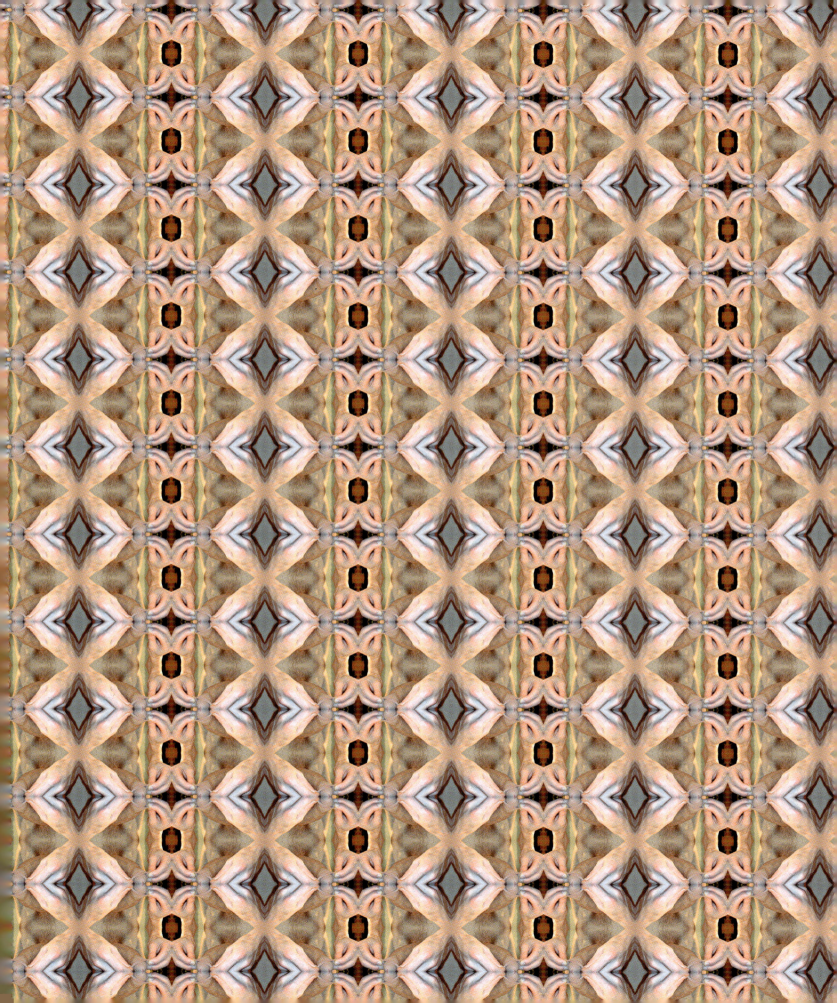

"Live long enough to find the right one"

Kate Sutton was commissioned by TBWA Paris to create a poster based on their award-winning film* for AIDES, an Aids charity based in France. The film is part of an awareness raising campaign, it tells the story of a girl who goes through different sex partners until she finds "the one". Sutton's work is deceptively simple, the movie content is extraordinarily condensed.

L'agence TBWA Paris a confié à Kate Sutton la création d'une affiche basée sur son court-métrage* réalisé pour l'association caritative française AIDES. Ce film fait partie d'une campagne pour la prise de conscience du risque de SIDA, il relate l'histoire d'une fille qui rencontre plusieurs partenaires sexuels avant de trouver « le bon». La simplicité du travail de Sutton est trompeuse, le contenu du film y est extraordinairement condensé.

Kate Sutton kreeg van TBWA Paris de opdracht een poster te ontwerpen, gebaseerd op de bekroonde film* die ze maakten voor AIDES, een Franse Aidsvereniging. De film maakt deel uit van een bewustmakingscampagne en gaat over een meisje dat verschillende seksuele partners heeft tot ze "de ware" vindt. Suttons werk is bedrieglijk simpel, de filminhoud buitengewoon gecondenseerd.

*It places emphasis on the search for a sexually compatible mate, which is unusual, and also features an interesting lead-in from childhood into teenage-hood. See it at www.aides.org/baby-baby/
*Inhabituel, ce court-métrage met l'accent sur la recherche d'un partenaire sexuellement compatible, il comporte aussi une introduction intéressante traitant du passage de l'enfance à l'adolescence. Voir www.aides.org/baby-baby/
*De nadruk ligt op de zoektocht naar een seksueel gepaste partner, hetgeen ongebruikelijk is; de interessante inleiding toont de overgang van kind naar puber. Te bekijken op www.aides.org/baby-baby/

Designer: Kate Sutton **Year:** 2006
Webmail: www.sleepycow.com

Penis Pixie, Bondage Bear, Rubber Duck, Saint Sebastianna

Trevor Brown candidly speaks of his technical shortcomings as a painter, but knows where the power of his images lies. "The concept, composition or the combination of elements (unexpected juxtapositions?) effecting a perceived 'shock value'? I think what separates me from other artists aiming for the same effect is that my intent is not actually shock but beauty (so, yes, my images are painted with love)." In keeping with his work, he makes no attempt to validate his fantasy—world explorations on a conceptual level—and does so in a very articulate manner.

S'il parle avec candeur de ses lacunes techniques en peinture, Trevor Brown sait en revanche où réside le pouvoir de ses images. « Le concept, la composition ou la combinaison d'éléments (des juxtapositions inattendues?) opèrent-ils une "valeur choc" perçue? A mon avis, ce qui me distingue des autres artistes à la recherche du même effet, c'est que mon intention n'est pas de choquer, mais de trouver la beauté (donc oui, je peins mes images avec amour) ». Conformément à ses travaux, il ne cherche pas à valider ses explorations imaginaires sur un plan conceptuel — et il exprime très clairement sa démarche —.

Trevor Brown heeft het losjes over zijn technische tekortkomingen als schilder, maar kent maar al te goed de kracht van zijn beelden. "Het concept, de compositie of de combinatie van elementen (onverwachte nevenschikkingen?) met als effect een voelbare 'shockwaarde'? Ik denk dat ik me van andere artiesten die hetzelfde effect zoeken onderscheid, omdat ik niet de shock maar de schoonheid zoek (dus, ja, mijn beelden zijn met liefde geschilderd)." In zijn werk probeert hij zijn exploraties van de fantasiewereld niet op een conceptueel niveau te valideren, maar legt hij het in tegendeel allemaal klaar en duidelijk uit.

Designer: Trevor Brown **Year:** 2004, 2005
Webmail: www.pileup.com/babyart **Photo:** Trevor Brown

TREVOR BROWN

RUBBER DOLL

23 ~ 28 JANUARY 2007

GALLERY LE DECO 5 • SHIBUYA • TOKYO

Metal

Hide'n'Peek bed

Wright wanted to make a piece of furniture that would create a strong emotional response. What carries more emotional weight than a bed? The traditional four-poster especially appealed to her because it concretizes the unconscious needs and desires naturally associated with the bed: sexuality, comfort, and protection. From the outside, its glimmering surface offers almost complete concealment, which creates curiosity and fires the imagination. The inside is a protected, sensuous space, a feeling that is heightened by the curtain's tactile, heavy aluminium beads.

Wright souhaitait créer un meuble capable de susciter une forte réaction émotionnelle. Quel meuble porte une plus grande charge émotionnelle que le lit? Son choix s'est arrêté sur le traditionnel baldaquin qui, à ses yeux, concrétise des besoins et des désirs inconscients – sexualité, confort et protection – qui y sont associés. Vue de l'extérieur, sa surface étincelante assure le secret quasi absolu, éveillant ainsi la curiosité et enflammant l'imaginaire. À l'intérieur, on découvre un espace protegé et sensuel, impression accentuée par la lourdeur et le caractère tactile des billes en aluminium du rideau perlé.

Wright wilde een meubelstuk maken dat op een sterk emotionele respons kon rekenen. En wat is er emotioneel meer geladen dan een bed? Het traditioneel hemelbed sprak haar bijzonder aan, omdat het onbewuste wensen en verlangens uitbeeldt, die van nature uit met het bed geassocieerd worden: seksualiteit, comfort en bescherming. De glinsterende buitenkant biedt een bijna perfecte schuilplaats, hetgeen nieuwsgierigheid opwekt en tot de verbeelding spreekt. De binnenkant is een beschermde, sensuele ruimte, versterkt door de zware aluminium parels van het gordijn.

Designer: Gala Wright for Viable **Year:** 2006
Webmail: www.viablelondon.com **Photo:** Mark Whitfield

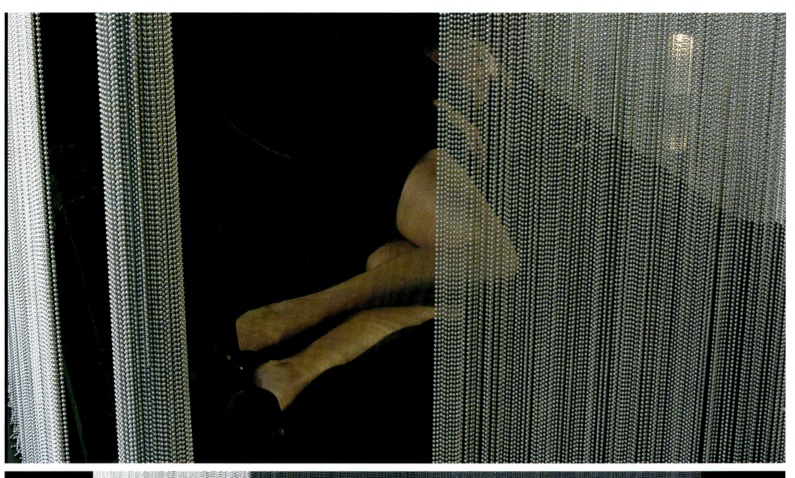

Necklaces

Erica Weiner uses inexpensive materials to make affordable jewellery that doesn't look cheap. Although she uses a lot of found or mass-produced objects, her work always feels personal. Her collection looks like it was created by an intuitively discerning personality, yet her pieces will endorse a story of your own, they are evocative without being too rigid. These Pelvis and Penis bone necklaces are just that, a contemporary version of His and Hers pendants.

Erica Weiner travaille à partir de matériaux bon marché pour créer des bijoux qui restent abordables sans avoir l'air toc. Tout en utilisant bon nombre d'objets trouvés ou fabriqués en série, ses créations conservent leur personnalité, On ressent à travers cette collection une créatrice dotée d'un sens de discernement intuitif, et ses bijoux adhéreront sans difficulté à votre propre histoire. Ils sont évocateurs, sans être trop rigides. Les colliers Os Pelvis et Os Penis sont exactement cela, une version contemporaine de pendentifs Elle et Lui.

Erica Weiner gebruikt betaalbare materialen voor juwelen die er niet goedkoop uitzien. Ook al werkt ze veel met op grote schaal gefabriceerde voorwerpen, haar werk voelt altijd persoonlijk aan. Haar collectie is duidelijk het werk van een scherpzinnige persoonlijkheid en toch zullen haar stukken ook bij jouw eigen verhaal aansluiten. Ze zijn indringend, zonder stug te zijn. Deze benen halssnoeren, Pelvis en Penis, zijn daar een voorbeeld van, een eigentijdse versie van de Hij en Zij hangertjes.

Designer: Erica Weiner **Year:** 2006
Webmail: www.ericaweiner.com **Photo:** Erica Weiner

Condom box

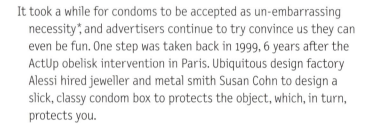

It took a while for condoms to be accepted as un-embarrassing necessity*, and advertisers continue to try convince us they can even be fun. One step was taken back in 1999, 6 years after the ActUp obelisk intervention in Paris. Ubiquitous design factory Alessi hired jeweller and metal smith Susan Cohn to design a slick, classy condom box to protects the object, which, in turn, protects you.

Il a fallu un certain temps pour que le préservatif devienne une nécessité et ne suscite plus l'embarras*, et les publicitaires s'acharnent à nous convaincre qu'il peut même être amusant. Un pas fut franchi en 1999, six ans après l'intervention d'ActUp sur l'Obélisque à Paris. Alessi, manufacture de design omniprésente, a confié à la bijoutière et orfèvre Susan Cohn le dessin d'une boîte à préservatifs élégante et raffinée. Ainsi, ces objets qui assurent votre protection sont à leur tour protégés.

Het duurde even voor condooms van hun taboes afraakten* en reclamemakers doen nog steeds hun best om ons ervan te overtuigen dat ze zelfs leuk kunnen zijn. Een belangrijke stap hierin dateert uit 1999, 6 jaar na de ophefmakende obeliskactie in Parijs. De alomtegenwoordige designfabrikant Alessi trok juwelier en metaalsmid Susan Cohn aan om een keurig, klassiek condoomdoosje te ontwerpen, een bescherming voor je eigen bescherming.

*Still arguably so, especially for teenagers- then again, while sex itself is considered embarrassing, how could it be otherwise?
*Bien que ceci soit discutable, en particulier chez les adolescents; mais tant que le sexe même demeure un sujet embarrassant, comment pourrait-il en être autrement?
*Nog steeds moeilijk, vooral bij pubers, maar hoe kan het ook anders als seks op zich een taboe is?

Designer: Susan Cohn for Alessi **Year:** 1999
Webmail: www.cohnartist.com, www.alessi.com **Photo:** Alessi

Big Boy is back from Istanbul

Albane Courtière does not want to be mistaken for a feminist. She likes it when things are clear, and right now, she thinks that there is a big mess between men and women. While in today's western world, her pieces may seem ironic or critical, she is, in fact, touched by the notion of manhood, and has great respect for it. She says, this is "a necklace, that women wear around the neck as a charm, they feel the phallus next to their breast, they can touch it, and after they feel better, they feel strong, because they are next to their men".

Albane Courtière ne souhaite pas qu'on la prenne pour une féministe. Elle aime que les choses soient claires et trouve la situation actuelle entre hommes et femmes est très confuse. Bien que ses créations puissent paraître ironiques, voire critiques dans le monde occidental d'aujourd'hui, elle est en réalité très sensible à la notion de masculinité, pour laquelle elle ressent un profond respect. Pour elle, cet objet est « un collier que la femme porte autour du cou comme une amulette, elle ressent la présence du phallus contre sa poitrine, elle peut le toucher et après cela elle se sent mieux, elle se sent forte car son homme est auprès d'elle ».

Albane Courtière wil niet voor feministe doorgaan. Ze houdt ervan als dingen duidelijk en direct zijn en is van mening dat er tussen man en vrouw veel rotzooi bestaat. Hoewel haar werk in de huidige westerse wereld ironisch of kritisch kan overkomen, is ze in feite getroffen door het begrip mannelijkheid en heeft ze er veel respect voor. Ze zegt: "Dit is een halssnoer dat vrouwen dragen als bezwering; ze voelen de fallus nabij hun borsten, ze kunnen hem aanraken en voelen zich daarna beter en sterker, omdat ze vlakbij hun man zijn."

Designer: Albane Courtière **Year:** 2006
Webmail: www.albanecourtiere.com **Photo:** Serge Anton

72 Degrees

"Quick, hide your porn!" 72 degrees* was designed with teenagers in mind. A bedroom shelf designed to provide a safe place to hide and store pornographic magazines, it has a secret compartment that can only be opened thanks to its key/ring. 72 degrees might prove difficult to sell at IKEA, so the designers thought it could be awarded by a leading pornographic magazine every month, and arrive at the family home in an inconspicuous package addressed to the lucky winner.

« Vite, cache ton porno »! C'est en pensant aux adolescents que l'étagère 72 Degrees* a été conçue. Cachette parfaite pour dissimuler ses magazines porno, elle a un compartiment secret qui s'ouvre au moyen d'une bague-clef. Réalisant que l'étagère se vendrait difficilement chez IKEA, les designers ont pensé à un autre moyen de diffusion : chaque mois, un tirage au sort organisé par l'un des grands magazines pornographiques attribuerait une 72 Degrees à l'un de ses lecteurs. Le cadeau serait livré sous pli discret à l'heureux gagnant.

"Vlug, stop die porno weg!" 72 degrees* werd voor pubers ontworpen. Het is een boekenplank met een veilig plaatsje om pornobladen in weg te stoppen, dankzij een geheim vakje dat enkel met een ringsleutel open kan. 72 degrees is niet bepaald een IKEA-product, dus stelden de designers voor het maandelijks als prijs te laten uitreiken door een leidinggevend pornoblad en het zo in een onschuldig pakketje bij de winnaar thuis binnen te smokkelen.

*72 degrees is the average angle of a healthy erection. The hidden compartment opens to this angle.
*72 degrés est l'angle moyen d'une érection saine. Le compartiment s'ouvre à cet angle.
*72 graden is de gemiddelde hoek van een gezonde erectie. En de openingshoek van het verborgen vakje.

Designer: Studio de Winter Leung **Year:** 2006
Webmail: www.studioleung.com,
www.studioleung.com/enjoie_design.htm

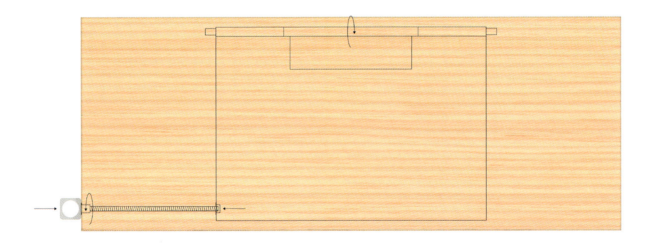

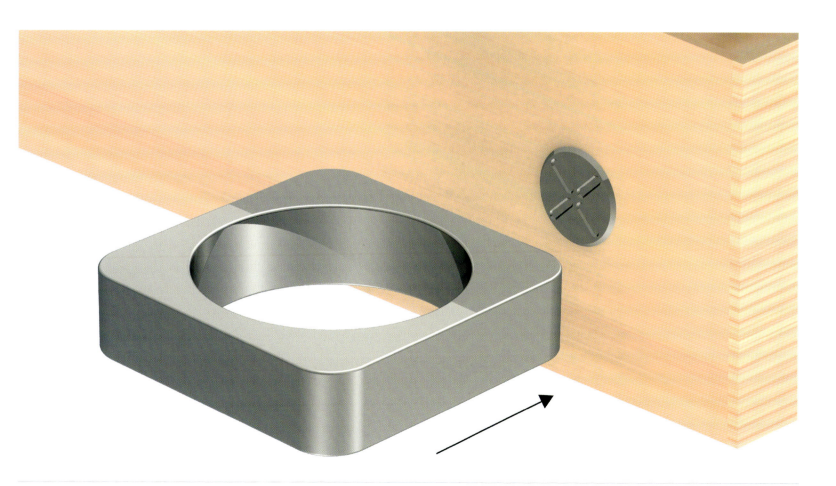

Risky business

Paul Derrez is very active in the contemporary jewellery scene, both as a jeweller and as a gallery owner*. In 1996, the "Risky Business" series and its unmistakable aesthetic became very popular, especially in the gay subculture. "Risky Business" refers to the act of showing one's own vulnerability. Interestingly enough, these pieces look everything but. Shiny, hard and sometimes pierced, they assert themselves fully, both as bold jewellery for men and as overtly sexual objects.

Paul Derrez est très actif dans le monde de la bijouterie contemporaine, aussi bien en tant que bijoutier qu'en tant que galeriste*. Sa collection « Risky Business », lancée en 1996, se distingue par un design très caractéristique qui lui a valu un grand succès auprès du milieu gai en particulier – l'expression « Risky Business » faisant référence à l'action de révéler sa propre vulnérabilité –. Note intéressante, ces objets paraissent tout sauf vulnérables. Brillants, durs, parfois percés, ils affirment leur propre existence en tant que bijoux pour homme et comme objets à connotation ouvertement sexuelle.

Paul Derrez is zeer actief in de hedendaagse juweliersbusiness, als juwelier en galeriehouder*. In 1996 was de "Risky Business"-reeks en diens onmiskenbare esthetica erg populair, in het bijzonder in de gay-subcultuur. "Risky Business" gaat over het tonen van je eigen kwetsbaarheid. Maar het interessante is dat deze stukken er helemaal niet zo uit zien. Glanzend, hard en soms voorzien van piercings, bevestigen ze zichzelf volkomen als krachtige mannelijke juwelen en openlijk seksuele objecten.

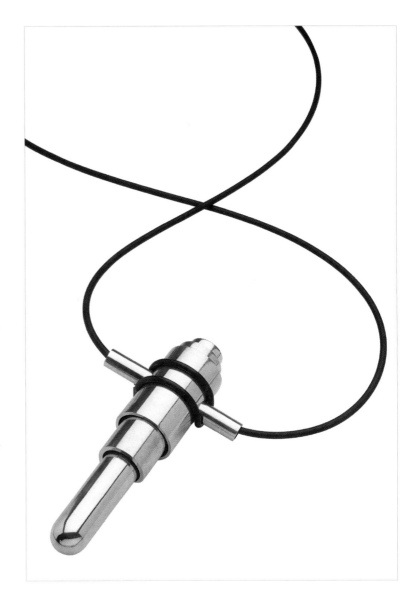

*Galerie Ra in Amsterdam is one of the leading spaces in its field.
*La Galerie Ra à Amsterdam fait figure de proue dans son domaine.
*Galerie Ra in Amsterdam is toonaangevend in de kunstsector.

Designer: Paul Derrez **Year:** 1996
Webmail: www.galerie-ra.nl **Photo:** Ton Werkhoven

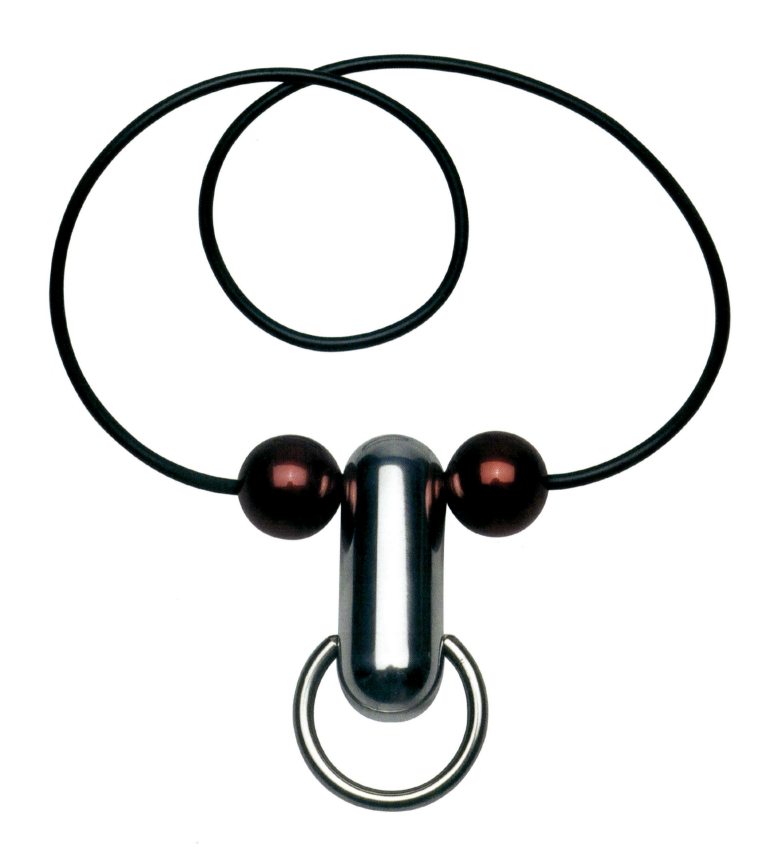

OhMiBod

The OhMiBod is a DJs wet dream. The ultimate experimental playground for music lovers, this vibrator's motions depend on the kind of music you listen to, and its intensity varies with volume, thus delivering all kinds of orgasms (musically curious people will reap the benefits of their open minds, it seems). The OhMiBod website also features user's posts, playlists, special mixes... The product is not endorsed by Apple Computers Inc., but the site boasts a partnership with the Apple®iTunes®Store, and founder Suki is an ex-Apple® product marketer.

Le OhMiBod est un rêve érotique pour DJ. Terrain d'expérimentation ultime pour amateurs de musique, ce vibromasseur réagit en fonction du type de musique que l'on joue et son intensité augmente avec le volume, décochant ainsi orgasmes en tout genre. Il semblerait que les plus musicalement curieux d'entre nous allons récolter le fruit de notre ouverture d'esprit. Les utilisateurs OhMiBod peuvent poster leurs messages, playlists et leurs propres mix sur le site web. Le produit n'est pas approuvé par Apple Computers Inc., cependant, sa créatrice Suki est une ex du marketing produit de chez eux, et le site s'enorgueillit d'un partenariat avec l'Apple®iTunes®Store.

OhMiBod is de natte droom van elke DJ. Deze vibrator is het toppunt van experimenteel speelgoed voor muziekliefhebbers, want zijn bewegingen en intensiteit veranderen naar gelang de muziek, met allerlei orgasmevarianten als resultaat (muzikaal nieuwsgierigen kunnen nu de opbrengst van hun ruimdenkendheid oogsten). Op de website van OhMiBod vind je ook recensies, playlists en speciale mixen. Het product is niet van de Apple Computers Inc., maar de site gaat prat op een overeenkomst met de Apple®iTunes®Store en oprichter Suki is een ex-Apple® productmarketeer.

Designer: OhMiBod **Year:** 2006
Webmail: www.ohmibod.com **Photo:** OhMiBod

Photo

Go Further

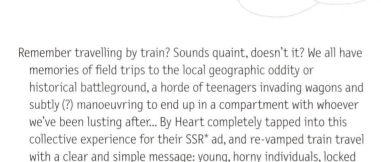

Remember travelling by train? Sounds quaint, doesn't it? We all have memories of field trips to the local geographic oddity or historical battleground, a horde of teenagers invading wagons and subtly (?) manoeuvring to end up in a compartment with whoever we've been lusting after... By Heart completely tapped into this collective experience for their SSR* ad, and re-vamped train travel with a clear and simple message: young, horny individuals, locked up in a small space far, far away from home.

Vous souvenez-vous de l'époque où l'on voyageait en train? Ça paraît désuet, non? Nous avons tous des souvenirs de sorties de classe au site d'intérêt géographique ou au champ de bataille historique du coin, une horde d'adolescents prenant les wagons d'assaut, s'arrangeant subrepticement (?) pour se retrouver dans le compartiment de la personne convoitée... C'est de cette expérience collective que l'agence By Heart s'est inspirée pour sa publicité SSR*, qui remet au goût du jour les voyages ferroviaires avec un message sans ambiguïté : des jeunes excités, enfermés dans un espace clos, bien loin de chez eux.

Weet je nog, die treinreizen? Klinkt lekker ouderwets, niet? We herinneren ons allemaal wel een schoolreis naar een plaatselijke bezienswaardigheid, met een troep pubers die de wagons binnenvallen en subtiel (?) manoeuvreren om met het voorwerp van hun begeerte in hetzelfde compartiment terecht te komen. By Heart haakt in op deze collectieve ervaring met hun reclamecampagne voor de SSR*. De boodschap is klaar en duidelijk: jonge, geile individuen, opgesloten in een kleine ruimte, heel ver van huis.

*Now STA, Student Travel Association.
*Association de promotion de voyages pour étudiants, aujourd'hui rebaptisée STA.
*Nu STA, Student Travel Association.

Designer: By Heart **Year:** 2001
Webmail: www.byheart.ch **Photo:** Diana Scheunemann

Our creative comes from within

smashLAB's homepage reads: "You aren't going to like us. smashLAB isn't like most other design firms. We aren't fun or stylish. Our design is practical and efficient. With that out of the way, why don't you press some of our buttons?" Which pretty much sums up their spirit, fiercely independent and completely un-frilly. A breath of fresh air in these neo-baroque times, the people at smashLAB had the courage to cut to the chase with their own ballsy ad campaign. Only one of four instalments is shown here, now go Google the other ones.

Page d'accueil du site de smashLAB: « On ne va pas vous plaire. smashLAB ne ressemble pas aux autres agences de design. Nous ne versons pas dans le fun ou le branché. Notre approche du design est pratique et fonctionnelle. Maintenant que nous sommes au clair, venez donc nous chercher. » Cette introduction résume assez bien l'esprit farouchement indépendant et sans chichis qui règne ici. Une bouffée d'air frais en notre époque néo baroque, les gens de smashLAB ont eu le courage d'aller droit au but avec une campagne de pub bien gonflée. Il y en a quatre en tout, Googlez donc les trois autres.

Op smashLAB's homepage lezen we: "Je gaat ons niet leuk vinden. smashLAB is anders dan de meeste designfirma's. We zijn niet grappig of stijlvol. Ons design is praktisch en efficiënt. Nu dit duidelijk is, kan je misschien doorklikken." Een goede samenvatting van hun karakter, extreem onafhankelijk en volledig tierelantijntjesloos. Als een hapje frisse lucht in deze tijden van neo-barok, hadden de mensen van smashLAB het lef er met een eigen pittige reclamecampagne tegenaan te gaan. Hier tonen we slechts één van de vier advertenties, dus google de anderen maar even op.

OUR CREATIVE COMES FROM WITHIN. smashLAB

Designer: smashLAB **Year:** 2005
smashLABPhoto: smashLAB

119

Winterzaad,
la semence d'hiver

When asked about this ad, the boys at Milk and Cookies* explained
that they found themselves without a season's greeting card in
sight, and that they "quickly shot this". Should all improvised
projects come out so well. Subtitle for the picture: "la quête de la
semence d'hiver parfaite", which translates to, "the quest for the
perfect winter semen". A nice example of Belgium's typically
cheeky, subversive humour- and an enticement to go check out
their cool website.

Interrogés sur l'origine de cette pub, les designers de Milk and
Cookies* ont expliqué qu'ils se sont retrouvés à Noël sans carte
de vœux, et que donc ils avaient « rapidement dû faire cette
séance photo ». L'improvisation à parfois du bon. Le résultat,
intitulé « la quête de la semence d'hiver parfaite », est un bon
exemple de cet humour belge typiquement effronté et subversif,
et c'est également une invitation à visiter leur excellent site web.

Volgens de jongens van Milk and Cookies* ontstond deze foto toen
ze geen kerstkaart klaar hadden en dus maar "snel dit in elkaar
flansten". Waren alle geïmproviseerde projecten maar zo geslaagd!
Ondertiteling bij de afbeelding: "la quête de la semence d'hiver
parfaite", oftewel, "zoektocht naar het perfecte winterzaad". Een
leuk voorbeeld van de typische, gedurfde, subversieve Belgische
humor en een verleidelijke uitnodiging om hun coole website te
bekijken.

*Self described "graphic design pimps, flash moguls, sex slaves to Gwen Stefani, McDo
addicts…"
*Qui se décrivent eux-mêmes comme « des macs du graphisme, des magnats de Flash,
esclaves sexuels de Gwen Stefani, et accros au McDo… »
*Beschrijven zichzelf als "grafisch designpooiers, flashmogols, seksslaven van Gwen
Stefani, McDonaldsgekken,…

Designer: Milk and Cookies **Year:** 2006
Webmail: www.milkandcookies.be **Photo:** Kurt Stallaert & Milk and Cookies

120

Porn cover art

alaska! is a good graphic designer who makes, amongst other things, covers art for alt-porn* movies. His work does not give you the creepy impression that smut is all there is to his life, or that he spends his time locked up in a possibly dark, possibly damp place, possibly using his own bodily fluids to glue his collages together. On the contrary, his work is fresh, and contributes to the credibility of the genre.

alaska! est un bon graphiste qui réalise, entre autres, des couvertures de films alt-porn*. Son travail ne donne pas l'impression glauque qu'il n'y a que le cul dans la vie, ni qu'il passe toute sa journée enfermé dans une pièce sombre et humide, utilisant ses propres fluides corporels pour réaliser ses collages. Au contraire, la fraîcheur qui s'en dégage contribue à la crédibilité du genre.

alaska! is een grafisch designer van onder andere kunstcovers voor alternatieve pornofilms*. Zijn werk geeft je niet die akelige indruk dat hij een schamel leven lijdt, opgesloten op een waarschijnlijk donkere, vochtige kamer, en zijn eigen lichaamsvochten gebruikt om zijn collages te plakken. Het is in tegendeel fris werk dat het genre geloofwaardig maakt.

*Alternative Pornography: mainly online medium usually featuring people belonging to "subcultures", often considered woman friendly and sex-positive.
*Alternative Pornography : Médium que l'on trouve surtout sur internet, mettant généralement en scène des personnes issues de milieux alternatifs, souvent considéré comme présentant une image positive du sexe et particulièrement respecteux/attrayant pour les femmes.
*Alternatieve pornografie: vooral online te vinden, gebruikt meestal personages uit "subculturen", is over het algemeen vrouwvriendelijk en geeft een positief beeld van seks.

Designer: alaska! **Year:** 2004, 2006, 2006
Webmail: www.sixmonthsoflight.com

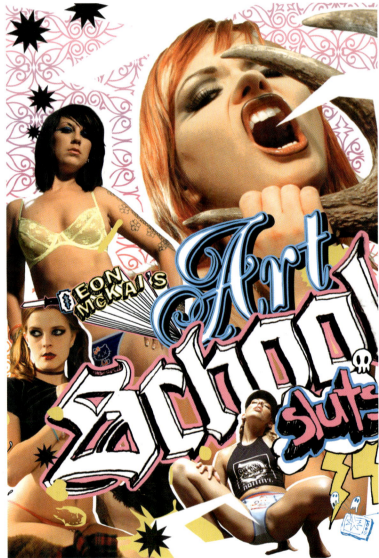

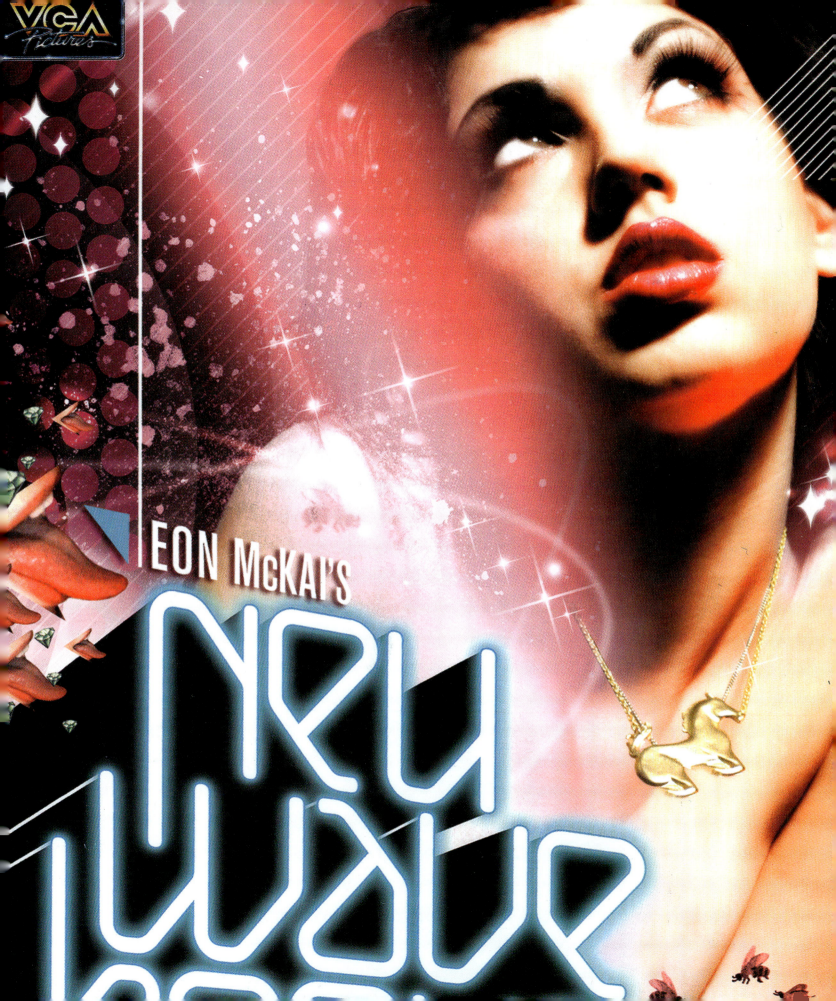

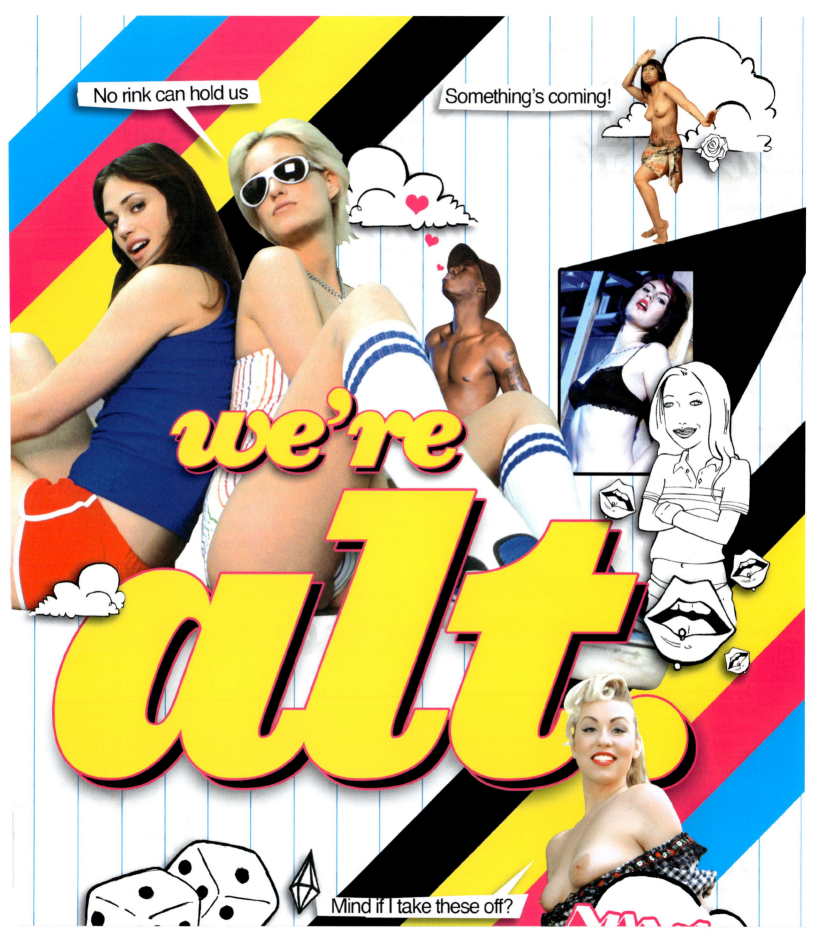

Impeach my bush

Where to start with Peaches. This woman's uncanny sense for associating or re-assigning words, images and sounds, can send people in a physical or intellectual frenzy at a moment's notice. Instinctive reactions spawn album titles such as "Fatherfucker", and "Impeach My Bush" (the promotion of which included a boy-beater rather than a wife-beater). In Tyler Shield's cover photos, we find her both stage-ready and un-sanitized- which, in this day and age, is a declaration of independence, and thus a sexual/political act in itself.

Par quoi commencer avec Peaches? Cette femme possède un sens inné pour associer ou détourner les mots, les images et les sons. Il lui suffit d'un instant pour susciter chez son public une véritable frénésie physique ou intellectuelle. Ses réactions instinctives engendrent des albums tels que « Fatherfucker » ou « Impeach My Bush ». Un de ses T-shirts de promotion était un marcel, appelé wife-beater en Anglais (*qui bat sa femme*), rebaptisé boy-beater (battant son homme, ou son fils) pour l'occasion. Sur les photos de Tyler Shields, nous la retrouvons à la fois mise en scène et non-aseptisée – ce qui constitue de nos jours une déclaration d'indépendance (et donc un acte sexuel et politique) en soi –.

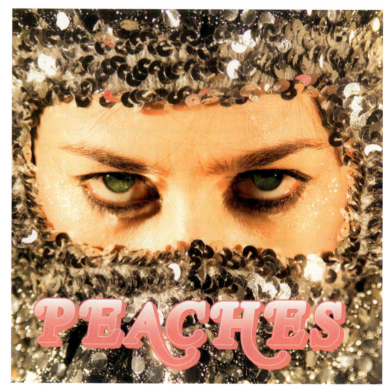

Hoe zouden we Peaches kunnen beschrijven? Deze vrouw kan zo griezelig goed woorden, beelden en geluiden associëren en herinterpreteren dat ze je in een wip tot fysieke of intellectuele waanzin kan drijven. Vol instinctieve reacties broedt ze albumtitels uit als "Fatherfucker" en "Impeach My Bush" (met als promotiegeschenk een sexy gay onderlijfje). Op de coverfoto's van Tyler Shield zien we haar zowel met als zonder make-up, hetgeen vandaag de dag reeds een onafhankelijkheidsverklaring is en dus een seksueel-politieke act op zich.

Designer: Peaches **Year:** 2006
Webmail: www.peachesrocks.com, www.tylershields.com
Photo: Tyler Shields

A1. Fuck Or Kill
A2. Boys Wanna Be Her
A3. Hit It Hard
A4. You Love It

B1. Two Guys (For Every Girl)
B2. Rock The Shocker
B3. Downtown

C1. Tent in Your Pants
C2. Do Ya
C3. Give 'er

D1. Slippery Dick
D2. Stick It To The Pimp
D3. Get It

Lapdancer

Beasley's photography avoids convolutions and aims for the core. This does not mean that they are thoughtless. When her pictures are bothersome, it is because they are too human- but it never seems like she "gets off on it", better said, they are never demeaning to their subject. A self-confessed colour-freak (pay close attention, behind the look of a snapshot, you will find a carefully colour-corrected picture), Beasley worked as a lapdancer for 8 years, coming to terms with her identity as a photographer, and documenting the world of strip-clubs.

Les photos de Beasley ne font pas de détours et vont droit au but— ce qui ne signifie pas pour autant qu'elles soient inconsidérées. Lorsque ses images dérangent, c'est qu'elles sont trop humaines. Pourtant, on à jamais l'impression que Beasley y prend son pied, autrement dit, elles ne sont jamais rabaissantes à l'égard du sujet. Folle de couleur avouée (regardez-y de près, derrière l'apparence d'un instantané, vous découvrirez une photo soigneusement retouchée), Beasley fut strip-teaseuse durant 8 ans, période durant laquelle elle apprît à accepter son identité de photographe, et à documenter le monde des boîtes de strip.

Beasley's fotografie gaat zonder omwegen naar de kern. Wat niet wil zeggen dat ze ondoordacht is. Haar foto's zijn wel eens hinderlijk omdat ze te menselijk zijn, maar het is nooit alsof ze er snel van af wil, ofwel, ze vernedert haar onderwerp niet. Beasley is naar eigen zeggen een kleurenfreak (kijk goed, de kleuren van wat een gewone snapshot lijkt, zijn in feite nauwkeurig bijgewerkt). Ze werkte 8 jaar als schootdanseres en verzoende dit met de fotografie in een verslag over de stripwereld.

Designer: Juliana Beasley **Year:** 2006
Webmail: www.julianabeasley.com **Photo:** Juliana Beasley

Blacklight Beauty

A different take on porn, a great cover. Jack the Zipper delivers his latest movie, named after a strip-club expression that refers to girls who only look good under a black light. This one features flashlit gangbangs in dark theatres, matching striped stockings and strap-ons, and clowns. It gets compared to a "circus fuckfest on acid" on every website we've visited, and to quote Gram Ponante: "Jack created a hybrid genre with Blacklight Beauty: a despair-laden art house gonzo with wacky recurring characters." Sure-fire cult status, inside and outside the industry.

Une vision différente du porno, du bon graphisme. Le titre du dernier film de Jack the Zipper s'inspire d'une expression de boîtes de striptease pour désigner les filles qui ne sont belles que sous les UV. Le film propose des orgies éclairées à la lampe de poche dans des salles de cinéma, des bas rayés et godemichés coordonnés, et des clowns. Sur tous les sites que nous avons visités, on en parle comme d'une « orgie au cirque sous acide ». Pour citer Gram Ponante, « Avec *Blacklight Beauty*, Jack a créé un genre hybride : un film d'art et d'essai déjanté, plein de désespoir, avec des personnages loufoques récurrents ». Futur statut culte, dans le monde du porno et au-delà.

Een andere kijk op porno, een prachtige cover. Jack the Zipper heeft voor zijn laatste film een strip-club uitdrukking als titel gekozen, die verwijst naar meisjes die er alleen bij blacklight goed uitzien. Gaat over neukpartijen bij flitslicht in donkere theaters, bijpassende gestreepte kousen en strap-ons en clowns. Alle websites die we bekeken hebben, maken de vergelijking met een "acid circus neukfestival" en om het met Gram Ponante te zeggen: "Jack creëerde met Blacklight Beauty een hybride genre: een cultfilm vol wanhoop en krankzinnige, steeds terugkerende personages." Hun cultstatus is verzekerd, zowel binnen als buiten de industrie.

Designer: Jack the Zipper **Year:** 2006
Webmail: www.jackthezipper.com **Photo:** Jack the Zipper

BLACKLIGHT BEAUTY

A JACKTHEZIPPER FILM

KLIGHT BEAUTY

JACKTHEZIPPER

BLACKLIGHT BEAUTY

design#2857

SPECIAL 2 DISC COLLECTORS EDITION!

FROM THE MOST DANGEROUS DIRECTOR IN XXX...JACKTHEZIPPER...
COMES THE MOST MINDBENDING PORNO FLICK YET...BLACKLIGHT BEAUTY...
FILLED WITH BACKROOM GANGBANGS...PUSSY WRESTLING...
UNFAITHFUL GIRLFRIENDS...ORAL FIXATION...PARAPHILIAS...
RANDY CIRCUS ACTS...EVEN DEATH...STARRING TWELVE OF
THE MOST SEXUALLY AGGRESSIVE WOMEN IN THE WORLD...
BLACKLIGHT BEAUTY IS ROCKING...JARRING...
HYPNOTIC...TWISTED...A SINEMATIC SMORGASBOARD
...FEAST ON IT!

PULSE PICTURES PRESENTS   THE NEXT JACKTHEZIPPER FILM   "BLACKLIGHT BEAUTY"   STARRING
FAITH   ALLIE SIN   JADE STARR   CHARLOTTE STOKELY   RILEY MASON   BREA BENNETT   CHARLIE LAINE   JOANNA ANGEL
ALICIA ALIGHOTTI   TARYN THOMAS   LORETTA LOREN   ROXY DEVILLE   ...AND A WHOLE LOTTA MEN

10 SIZZLING SEX SCENES DELETED SCENES AND OUTTAKES BTS DOCUMENTARY: *MAKING BLACKLIGHT* PHOTO SLIDESHOW 5.1 SURROUND SOUND
FETISH MENUS PLAYABLE WORLDWIDE   PULSEXXX.COM   BLACKLIGHTBEAUTY.COM   JACKTHEZIPPER.COM   ZIPPER FILMS   pulse   PUL502

8 58057 00111 8

pulse
PICTURES

Glass & ceramics

Villa Tinto

De Coninck hired Arne Quinze* to design a proper brothel in Antwerp. Visually, the result is a slightly impersonal mix of janitor-friendly surfaces and neo-baroque details (patterned ceilings, leopard bedspreads, braided leather whips...). On a practical level, we have a sophisticated alarm system, safes, en suite bathrooms, flattering window lights, an on-site police station, and hidden mirrors so the women can check out potential customers before opening their windows.

De Coninck a confié à Arne Quinze* la création d'un bordel à Anvers. Visuellement, cela donne un mélange relativement impersonnel de surfaces faciles à laver et de détails néo baroques (plafonds à motifs, couvre-lits en léopard, fouets en cuir tressé, etc.). Au niveau pratique, il y a un système d'alarme dernier cri, des coffres-forts, des chambres avec salles de bains attenantes, des éclairages flatteurs pour les vitrines, un poste de police et des miroirs dissimulés qui permettent aux dames de jeter un coup d'œil au client potentiel avant d'ouvrir (ou non) leur fenêtre.

De Coninck vroeg aan Arne Quinze* een eersteklas bordeel te ontwerpen in Antwerpen. Het resultaat is een visueel ietwat onpersoonlijke mix van onderhoudsvriendelijke materialen en neo-barrokke details (versierde plafonds, bedspreien met luipaardmotief, gevlochten leren zwepen...). Verder zorgde men voor een geraffineerd alarmsysteem, kluizen, en suite badkamers, flateuze raamverlichting, een eigen politiebureau en verborgen spiegels om de potentiële klanten te zien alvorens ze binnen te laten.

*Highly prestigious, resourceful and self-taught, co-founder of Quinze & Milan.
*Designer autodidacte prestigieux et ingénieux, cofondateur de Quinze & Milan.
*De prestigieuze, vindingrijke en autodidactische medeoprichter van Quinze & Milan.

Designer: Quinze & Milan **Year:** 2004
Webmail: www.quinzeandmilan.be **Photo:** Quinze & Milan

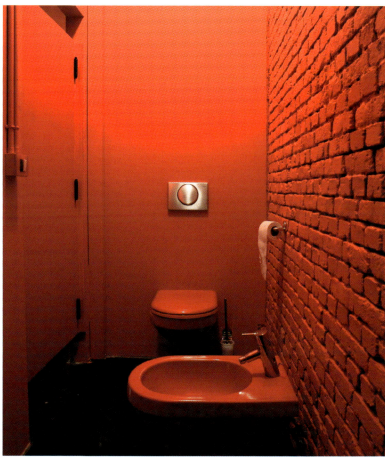

Erotic Pharmacy

You can finally set your lubricant or your massage oil on your dressing table without shame, in fact, it's the rest of your things that might look a bit dreary next to these sleek, dark glass bottles. Their explicit take on old school labels is only matched by their content: steeped in essential oils, these concoctions complement the body's natural scents (the Klitoris Climax Cream tastes like honey for example). Quoting Coco: "Rubber gloves and plenty of slippery, silky Gentleman's Relish make for the best warm handshake. Ever."

Vous pouvez enfin laisser traîner votre lubrifiant ou votre huile de massage sur la table de nuit sans la moindre gêne. Ce sont plutôt vos autres babioles qui paraîtront bien ternes à côté de ces élégants flacons de verre. Leurs noms et images explicites, apposés sur de vieilles étiquettes de genre pharmaceutique, n'ont d'égal que leur contenu : ces concoctions à base d'huile essentielle complètent les parfums naturels du corps (par exemple, la Klitoris Climax Cream a un goût de miel). Comme l'affirme Coco : « Une paire de gants en latex et une bonne dose d'huile soyeuse Gentleman's Relish assurent la plus chaleureuse des poignées de mains. De loin ».

Eindelijk kun je je glijmiddel en je massageolie zonder blozen op je toilettafel zetten. Alleen kunnen je andere spullen er dan wat saai uitzien naast deze strakke, donkere, glazen flesjes. De expliciete keuze voor ouderwetse schooletiketten past bij de inhoud: deze met etherische oliën doordrongen brouwsels vullen de natuurlijke geuren van het lichaam aan (de Klitoris Climax Cream proeft bv. naar honing). Zoals Coco zegt: "Rubberen handschoenen en een boel gladde, zijige Gentleman's Relish zorgen voor de beste warme handdruk ooit."

Designer: Coco de Mer **Year:** 2005
Webmail: www.coco-de-mer.co.uk **Photo:** Coco de Mer

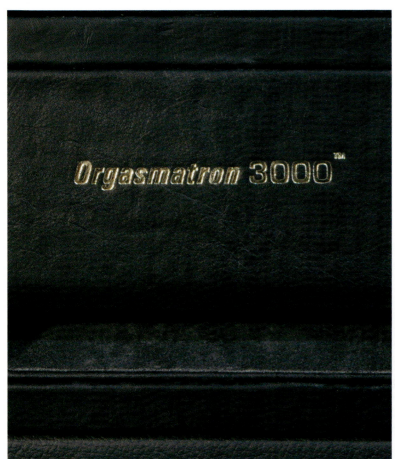

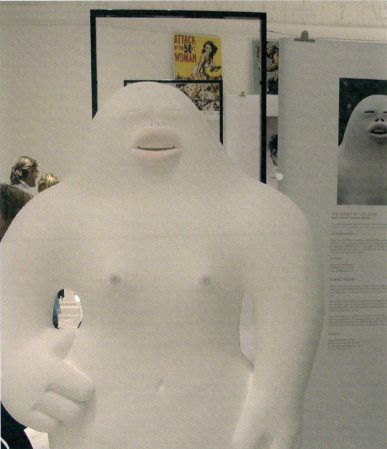

Bubble-up tiles

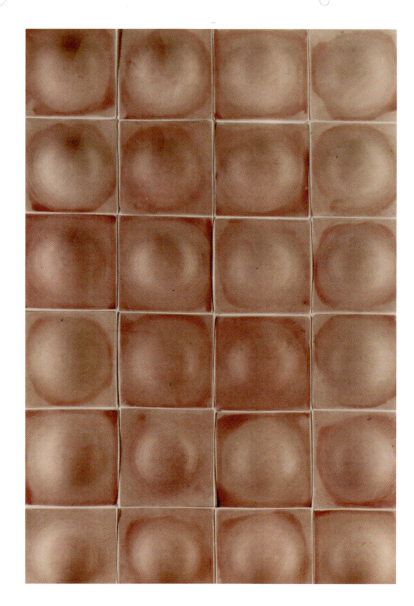

Esther Derkx is a Dutch product designer who likes to appose her "small interferences" to daily objects or found materials. She took inspiration in the "soft, friendly" forms of the human body and in ceramic's capacity to retain heat when designing the Bubble-up tiles. Their rounded shape and pink-tinted, glazed surface lends them a sensual and warm appearance. They are ideal for the bathroom. If you place them near or around your heater, they will capture the heat, and hold it for a longer period of time than regular tiles.

Designer produit, la Néerlandaise Esther Derkx prend un malin plaisir à apposer ses « petites interférences » à des objets du quotidien ou des matériaux de récupération. C'est en s'inspirant des formes « douces et chaleureuses » du corps humain, ainsi que de l'inertie thermique de la faïence, qu'elle a créé les carreaux Bubble-up. Leur rondeur et leur surface vernie de couleur rosée dégagent une impression de sensualité et de chaleur. Ces carreaux sont idéaux pour la salle de bains, si vous les placez près d'un radiateur, ils emmagasineront la chaleur et la restitueront beaucoup plus longtemps qu'une faïence classique.

Esther Derkx is een Nederlandse productdesigner die graag haar "kleine ingrepen" toepast op dagelijkse voorwerpen of gevonden materialen. Voor de Bubble-up tegels inspireerde ze zich op de "zachte, vriendelijke" vormen van het menselijk lichaam en op de warmtevastheid van ceramiek. Hun ronde vorm en rozige glazen oppervlak zijn sensueel en warm. Ze zijn ideaal voor de badkamer. Dicht bij de radiator houden ze de warmte langer vast dan normale tegels.

Designer: Esther Derkx **Year:** 2004
Webmail: www.estherx.nl **Photo:** Esther Derkx

Memento Mori pendant

Constanze Schreiber's new work is called *Abschiedsfest*: Farewell Party in German. This particular piece, Memento Mori*combines a modernity and straight-faced quirkiness. The imagery of two copulating flies contrasts with its serious pebble-like weight. The fact that it is obviously handmade encourages an emotional reading which leads the mind to these topics: sex, getting it while you can, break-ups, mourning, and new beginnings.

La nouvelle série de Constanze Schreiber s'intitule « Abschiedsfest » (« fête d'adieu » en allemand). Cette oeuvre, baptisée Memento Mori*, conjugue modernité et excentricité pince-sans-rire. L'image de deux mouches en train de copuler contraste avec le poids sérieux de l'objet, qui rappelle un galet. Le fait qu'il soit manifestement fait main invite à une lecture émotionnelle qui éveille l'esprit sur des thèmes tels que: l'amour, le faire pendant qu'il est temps, la séparation, le deuil et les nouveaux départs.

Het nieuwe werk van Constanze Schreiber heet "Abschiedsfest", afscheidsfeest in het Duits. Dit stuk in het bijzonder, Memento Mori*, combineert moderniteit en bloedserieuze spitsvondigheid. Het beeld van twee copulerende vliegen contrasteert met het serieuze, kiezelachtige steentje. Doordat het zichtbaar met de hand gemaakt is, is onze reactie emotioneel en denken we aan topics als: seks, pak wat je krijgen kan, scheidingen, treuren en opnieuw beginnen.

*"Remember that you are mortal" in Latin, it names a genre of artistic creation that aims to remind us of our own mortality.
*« Souviens-toi que tu es mortel » en latin, d'après un genre artistique qui a pour but de nous rappeler notre mort inéluctable.
*"Denk aan de dood" in het Latijn. Duidt op een artistiek genre dat ons aan onze sterfelijkheid wil herinneren.

Designer: Constanze Schreiber **Year:** 2006
Webmail: www.constanze-schreiber.ne **Photo:** Eddo Hartmann

DivinaDisco

A Pompeian homage to painting and naked ladies, this 300m² Milan club is punctuated with mosaic and digital-print odalisques*. Bisazza (an ultra-luxe, very design-conscious Italian mosaic manufacturer) and Fabio Novembre joined forces to re-create and showcase these famous paintings, including a huge, computerized tile version of Courbet's "L'Origine du Monde" above the bar.

Un hommage Pompéien à la peinture et aux femmes nues, cette boîte milanaise de 300 m² est ponctuée de mosaïques et d'odalisques* en impression numérique. Bisazza (manufacture de mosaïque italienne haut de gamme et très design) s'est associé à Fabio Novembre pour recréer et présenter ces œuvres célèbres, dont une immense version carrelée de *L'Origine du monde* de Courbet, créée par ordinateur, trônant au-dessus du bar.

Deze Milaanse club van 300m² is een Pompeiaanse hommage aan de schilderkunst en naakte dames, vol mozaïek en digitale odalisken*. Bisazza (een superluxueuze, zeer designbewuste, Italiaanse mozaïekfabricant) en Fabio Novembre besloten samen deze beroemde schilderijen te hercreëren en tentoon te stellen, inclusief een enorme, gecomputeriseerde tegelversie van Courbet's "L'Origine du Monde" boven de bar.

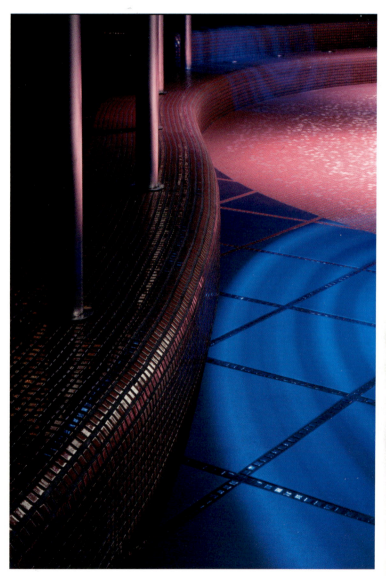

*Originally a virgin female slave, possibly rising to the role of wife or concubine, usually restricted to serving the harem. Came to mean "reclining figure" in art jargon.
*À l'origine une femme vierge, esclave au service d'un harem pouvant parfois accéder au rang d'épouse ou de concubine. Devenu partie du jargon artistique, désigne une femme allongée.
*Oorspronkelijk een maagdelijke slavin die tot echtgenote of concubine kon promoveren, maar meestal enkel de harem diende. In het kunstjargon verschoven naar "leunende figuur".

Designer: Fabio Novembre **Year:** 2001
Webmail: www.novembre.it **Photo:** Alberto Ferreo, Pasquale Formisano

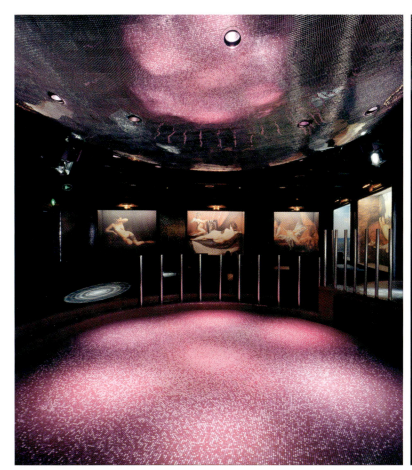

L'Origine du monde

Sexe by Accident

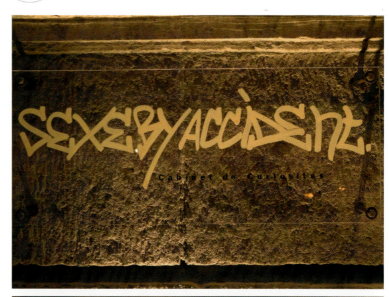

An offshoot of 20th century antiques shop Chic by Accident, Sexe by Accident is in keeping with owner Emmanuel Picault's realization that all his work is sexually charged. A collection of furniture and objects that throw us back to sensual pleasure, the concept is loaded with "endless possibilities which the gallery offers to explore with a sense of humour, of transgression, and, to top it all… good taste". Picault reveals the sexual pleasure that these objects, as creative endeavours, are automatically loaded with.

Rejeton de Chic by Accident, boutique d'antiquités du XXe siècle d'Emmanuel Picault, la galerie Sexe by Accident est née de sa prise de conscience que tout son travail est chargé de connotations sexuelles. Ensemble de meubles et d'objets qui renvoient aux plaisirs sensuels, le concept se définit par « les infinies possibilités que la galerie se propose d'explorer avec humour, transgression et, pour comble… bon goût ». Picault nous révèle le plaisir sexuel qui habite automatiquement ces objets en tant que fruits d'un effort créatif.

Sexe by Accident is een uitloper van de 20ste-eeuwse antiekwinkel Chic by Accident en past volledig in Emmanuel Picault's besef dat al zijn werk seksueel geladen is. Het gaat om een collectie meubels en voorwerpen die ons met sensueel genot overvallen, een concept vol "eindeloze mogelijkheden die je in de galerie kan verkennen met gevoel voor humor, overtreding en tenslotte… goede smaak". Picault onthult het seksuele genot waarmee deze voorwerpen, als de creatieve inspanningen die ze zijn, automatisch geladen zijn.

Designer: Emmanuel Picault **Year:** 2006
Webmail: www.chicbyaccident.com **Photo:** Fabien Tijou

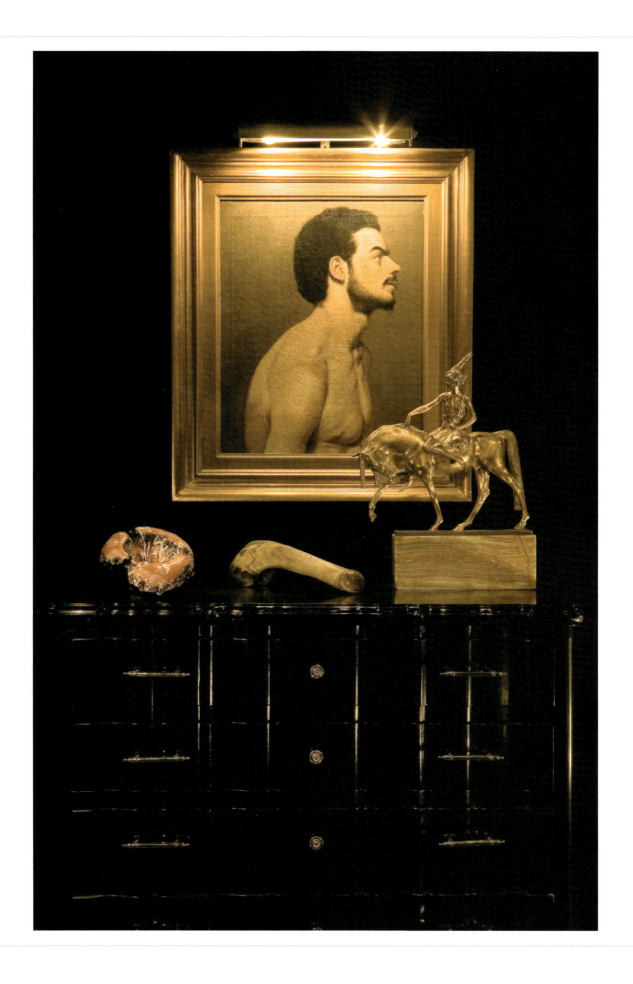

silk

Satin Tie-ups

One of Charlotte Semler and Nina Hampson's first decisions in setting up Myla was to ignore a focus-group session, which concluded that women usually associated sex shops with tarts and boudoirs. Apparently, Semler "decreed that these women simply couldn't comment on what they hadn't seen before so didn't necessarily know what they might want from sex". They bet on silk lingerie, real-pearl g-strings, and designer vibrators. These satin tie-ups epitomize Myla's reason for success: luxurious, playful, and as soft or hard as you want them to be.

En créant Myla, l'une des premières décisions de Charlotte Semler et de Nina Hampson fut d'ignorer les résultats d'une étude selon laquelle la plupart des femmes associent sex-shops et prostituées, ou boudoirs. Charlotte Semler aurait déclaré : « ces femmes ne peuvent pas se prononcer sur ce qu'elles n'ont jamais vu, et donc elles ne savent pas nécessairement ce qu'elles pourraient vouloir du sexe. » Les deux créatrices misèrent sur de la lingerie en soie, des strings en perles véritables et des vibromasseurs très design. Ces liens de satin illustrent parfaitement les raisons du succès de Myla : ils sont luxueux, ludiques, et aussi hard ou soft que l'envie du moment.

Toen Charlotte Semler en Nina Hampson met Myla begonnen, besloten ze geen acht te slaan op een doelgroepsessie waaruit bleek dat vrouwen een seksshop meestal met hoeren en bordelen associëren. Semler besliste "dat deze vrouwen eenvoudigweg niet konden oordelen over iets dat ze nooit gezien hadden en dus ook niet konden weten wat ze van seks verwachtten". Ze gaan voor zijden lingerie, g-strings met parels en design-vibrators. Deze satijnen tie-ups verklaren het succes van Myla: luxueus, speels en zo zacht of zo hard als je zelf wil.

Designer: Myla **Year:** 2004
Webmail: www.myla.com **Photo:** Myla

Bondage slip

Coco de Mer makes "ethically-sourced" sound sexy, and so it is. Sam Roddick created and runs it as a high-end, "woman-friendly" alternative to seedy sex shops, such as the ones you could find not far from its original location in London- "woman-friendly", and, unsurprisingly, men love to shop there too. These smart bondage knickers are great: no bedposts or fully furnished dungeons required, and as many positions as your mind, or body, can muster. They will give you tie-me-up fantasies if you don't already have them.

Les mots « commerce équitable » sont sexy dans la bouche de Coco de Mer. Cette société, créée et gérée par Sam Roddick, offre aux femmes une alternative accueillante et haut de gamme aux sex-shops mal famés, tels que ceux que l'on trouve dans le même quartier de Londres où se situait leur boutique d'origine- pensé pour les femmes, et, pas étonnant, les hommes aussi aiment y faire leurs emplettes. Ces culottes de bondage sont géniales. Tête de lit ou donjon tout équipé non-requis; et les seules limites sont celles de votre corps et de votre esprit. Si vous n'aviez pas encore de fantasmes bondage, ce n'était qu'une question d'accessoire.

Coco de Mer kan "ethisch geïnspireerd" sexy doen klinken. Sam Roddick ontwierp hiermee een vrouwvriendelijk alternatief van hoge kwaliteit voor de gore seksshops die de winkel in Londen omringen — vrouwvriendelijk, maar ook verrassend in trek bij mannen. Deze mooie bondage slip is fantastisch: weg met bedstijlen of volledig uitgeruste kerkers; probeer alle houdingen uit die je geest of lichaam aankunnen. Mocht je nooit bondage-fantasieën gehad hebben, dan krijg je die nu vast wel.

Designer: Coco de Mer **Year:** 2005
Webmail: www.coco-de-mer.co.uk **Photo:** Coco de Mer

Penis crest Quilt

Quilting usually conjures up images of sweet, arthritic grandmas
sitting in a circle at gaslight. This is a one-sided and outdated
image, from Sex and the City to the Golden Girls; it's difficult to
imagine anything that gets more irreverent then a group of
chatting women. This ruby red, penis crest, satin quilt is
handmade by a fair trade project in Turkey. Apart from loving the
thought of rolling around on it naked, we like to imagine the kind
of banter that went on while it was being made.

Le patchwork évoque le plus souvent une veillée de grands-mères
arthritiques assises en cercle à la lumière d'un bec de gaz.
Pourtant, c'est une image révolue, et plutôt arbitraire. De *Sex and
the City* au *Golden Girls*, il est difficile d'imaginer plus
irrévérencieux qu'une discussion entre femmes. Cet édredon de
satin rouge sang au blason pénis est fait main dans le cadre d'un
programme de commerce équitable en Turquie. Outre la douce
idée de se rouler dessus en tenue d'Eve, on se plaît à imaginer le
genre de plaisanteries qui ont dû accompagner sa réalisation.

Handgemaakte bedspreien doen meestal denken aan dingen als
schattige, jichtige oudjes bij gaslicht. Dat is een eenzijdig en
ouderwets beeld: na Sex and the City en The Golden Girls is het
moeilijk iets oneerbiedigers te bedenken dan een groep
babbelende vrouwen. Deze robijnrode bedsprei met peniskroon is
met de hand gemaakt door een fair-tradeproject in Turkije. Het
idee er naakt op rond te stoeien is zeker niet onaangenaam, maar
bedenk ook eens wat een lol de makers gehad moeten hebben.

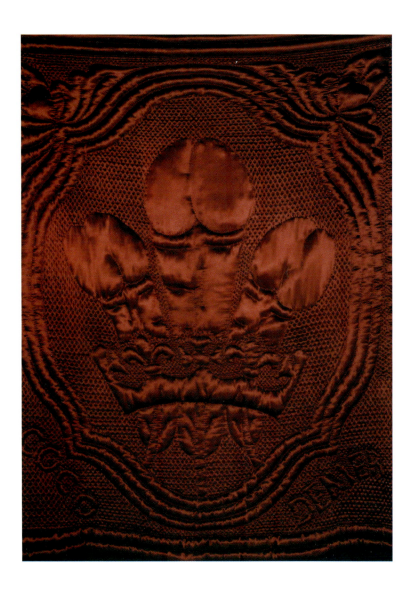

Designer: Coco de Mer **Year:** 2005
Webmail: www.coco-de-mer.co.uk **Photo:** Coco de Mer

Teach me a lesson ruler, Rose & Bird Cami and Knickers

According to regular practioners, wooden rulers, unlike crops and paddles, produce a hard, breath-taking sting, which is exactly the reason why some people are die-hard fans. Combine that with a deceptively sweet, frilly outfit, a pair of gloves from a more sophisticated era (imagine how your lover's skin would feel through that mesh...), and a strong choice in hosiery... You'll be demanding to be addressed as Miss Holloway* in no time.

D'après les spécialistes, la règle en bois diffère de la cravache ou de la palette en ceci qu'elle produit une douleur cinglante qui coupe le souffle, et c'est pour cette raison qu'elle fait des inconditionnels. Ajoutez-y une tenue en dentelle faussement innocente, une paire de gants issue d'une autre époque (imaginez la peau de votre amant à travers ce maillage...) et une paire de bas bien affirmée. Vous exigerez que l'on vous appelle Miss Holloway* en aussi peu de temps qu'il en faut pour le dire.

Volgens ervaren gebruikers geven houten latten, anders dan zwepen of peddels, een harde, adembenemende tik en hebben ze juist daarom zulke verstokte fans. Doe daar een bedrieglijk snoezig lijfje met volants bij, een paar handschoenen uit vervlogen tijden (beeld je in hoe de huid van je minnaar zal voelen door die mazen heen) en een brede keuze aan lingerie... Binnen de kortste keren wil je als Miss Holloway* aangesproken worden.

*Heroine of Steven Shainberg's exceptional "The Secretary", the story of two people coming together in unconventional harmony.
*Héroïne de l'exceptionnel *The Secretary* dirigé par Steven Shainberg, l'histoire d'un couple qui trouve une harmonie peu conventionnelle.
*Hoofdrolspeelster in Steven Shainberg's uitzonderlijke film "The Secretary", over twee personen die bij elkaar een bijzondere harmonie vinden.

Designer: Coco de Mer **Year:** 2005
Webmail: www.coco-de-mer.co.uk **Photo:** Coco de Mer

Laurel, Tae, Velvet, Marguerite, Dorita, Florrie, Margo, Amour de Tita

When you buy a pair of Miss Bellasis nipple tassels, you also receive the story of their creation. Unfortunately, we don't have the space for these stories here, but they are all great. The company was founded at the end of the last century. A recently divorced woman was moving to London, and her friend thought the only appropriate gift would be a pair of red sequin, heart-shaped nipple tassels- bless her. This led to more pairs, and so on. Every tassel is handmade to order, made with vegan materials, or fair-traded chocolate in the case of Amour de Tita.

Lorsque vous achetez un jeu de pompons de seins Miss Bellasis, vous recevez également leur histoire. Malheureusement, nous manquons de place pour vous les raconter toutes, mais sachez qu'elles sont extraordinaires. L'entreprise fut fondée à la fin du siècle dernier, lors du déménagement à Londres d'une dame récemment divorcée. Une amie souhaita lui offrir un cadeau à la hauteur de l'occasion, et lui fabriqua une paire de pompons de seins en paillettes rouges et en forme de cœur. Cette création fit boule-de-neige. Réalisée sur commande, chaque paire est confectionnée à partir de matériaux végétaliens, ou de chocolat issu de commerce équitable dans le cas du modèle Amour de Tita.

Als je je een paar tepelkwastjes van Miss Bellasis aanschaft, krijg je er meteen hun scheppingsverhaal bij. We hebben hier jammer genoeg geen plaats voor al die verhalen, maar ze zijn geweldig. Het bedrijf werd eind vorige eeuw opgericht. Een pas gescheiden vrouw verhuisde naar Londen en een vriendin vond geen gepaster cadeau dan een paar hartvormige tepelkwastjes met rode lovertjes – God zegene haar! Daar kwamen nog meer tepelkwasten van, enzovoorts. Elke kwast is op bestelling en met de hand gemaakt, van plantaardig materiaal, of fair-tradechocolade in het geval van Amour de Tita.

Designer: Miss Bellasis **Year:** 2004, 2005, 2006
Webmail: www.missbellasis.com **Photo:** David A Webb/Miss Bellasis

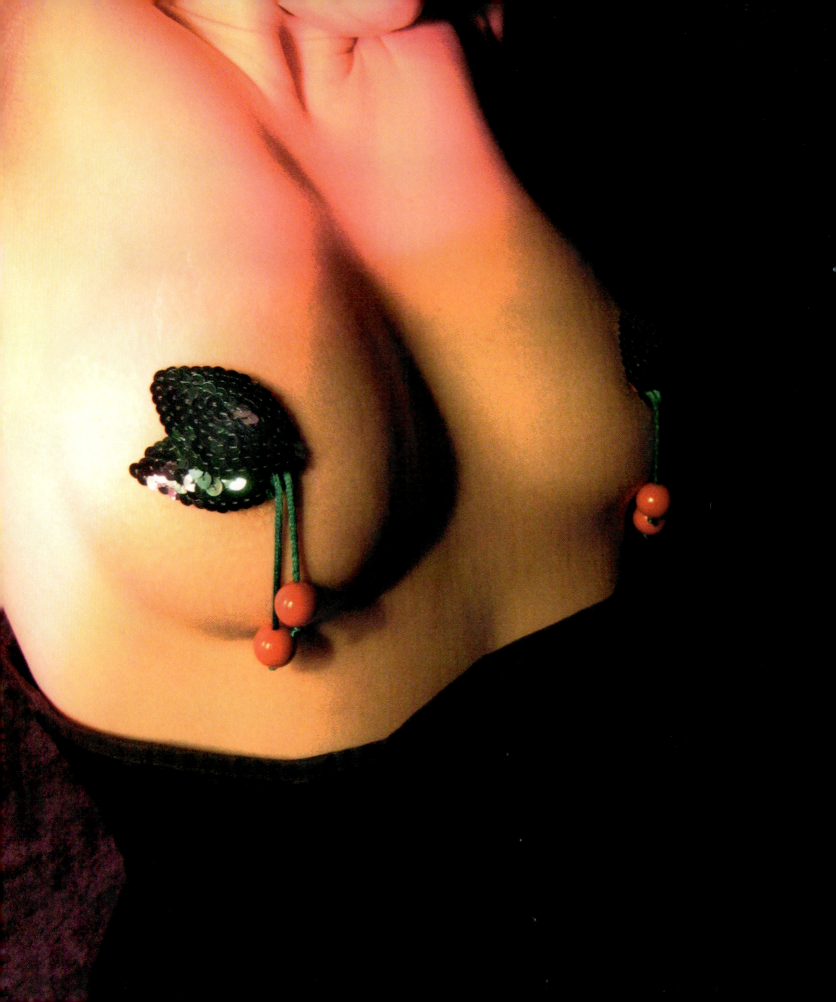

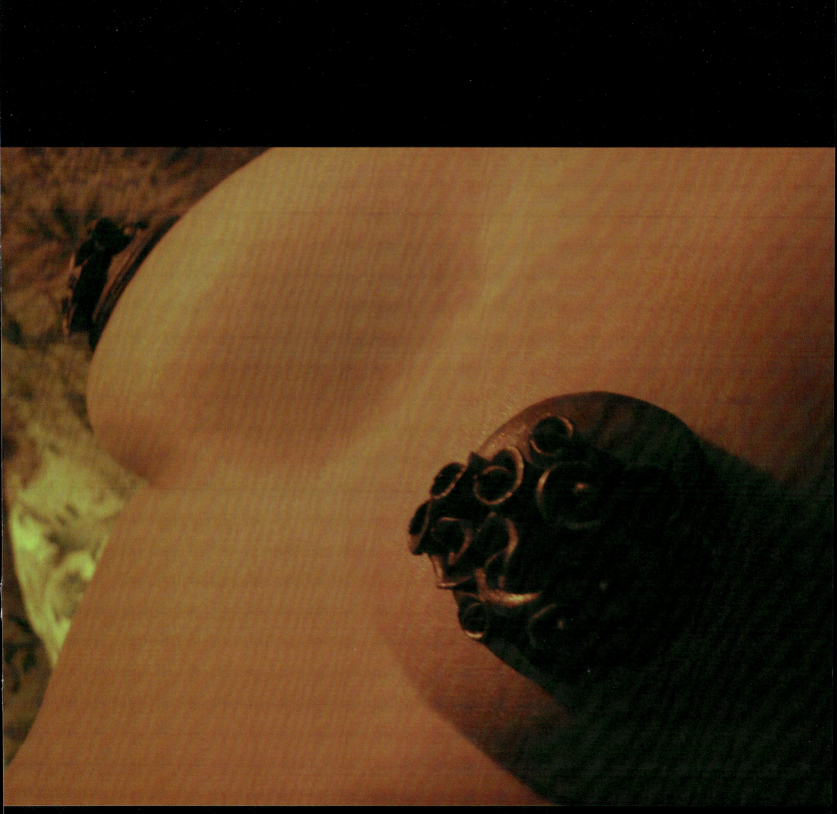

Big Boy bedcovers

These rabbit fur, cashmere, and silk bed covers refer to our collective unconscious. "Big boy dans sa belle auto", the phallus in his spanking new pink corvette, finds understanding in Miss Courtière: "Here you see a naive big boy with a lot of humour. We all know how most of men like cars. It is like us with dolls". The second bed cover, "Bonne Nuit les Petits", is a new take on an old children's TV show which featured a bear travelling on a cloud, wishing children a good night. Here, you find Big Boy on a cloud "giving tenderness to women before sleeping".

Ces couvre-lits en peau de lapin, en cachemire et en soie renvoient à notre inconscient collectif. « Big boy dans sa belle auto », le phallus dans sa rutilante Corvette rose flambant neuve, trouve grâce aux yeux d'Albane Courtière : « Vous voyez ici un grand garçon naïf et plein d'humour. Nous savons tous combien la plupart des hommes aiment l'automobile. C'est comme nous avec les poupées ». Le second couvre-lit, « Bonne Nuit les Petits », revisite un ancien programme télévisé dans lequel un ourson souhaitait bonne nuit aux enfants du haut de son nuage. Big Boy fait de même, il « donne de la tendresse aux femmes avant de s'endormir ».

Deze bedspreien uit konijnenvel, kasjmier en zijde verwijzen naar ons collectieve onderbewustzijn. Miss Courtière over "Big boy dans sa belle auto", de fallus in zijn spiksplinternieuwe, roze Corvette: "Je ziet hier een naïeve grote jongen met veel gevoel voor humor. We weten hoeveel de meeste mannen van auto's houden. Het is zoals wij met poppen". De tweede bedspri, "Bonne Nuit les Petits" is een nieuwe visie op een oud kinderprogramma met een beer die vanaf een wolk de kinderen welterusten zei. Hier zie je Big Boy op een wolk terwijl hij "tederheid schenkt aan vrouwen voor het slapengaan".

Designer: Albane Courtière **Year:** 2006
Webmail: www.albanecourtiere.com **Photo:** Serge Anton

Bling

Yva

Lelo's vibrators are amongst the most popular in the world. You can find them in almost every sex or erotic lifestyle shop, and yet the classic Néa model and its smooth handful of a shape still feels, and looks like an intimate object. A classic form, this 18k gold number looks like a little Brancusi. Since metal retains temperature, the golden Néa and its stainless steel counterpart can weigh down on your skin like a pound of chilled caviar, or the warm hand of a stranger, depending on your inclinations.

Les vibromasseurs Lelo sont parmi les plus populaires au monde. Ils se trouvent dans quasiment tous les sex-shops et boutiques d'accessoires érotiques, et pourtant, leur classique Néa, caractérisé par sa forme et son toucher délicats, n'a rien perdu de son caractère intime. Cet instrument aux formes classiques et doré à l'or 18 carats ressemble à un petit Brancusi. Le métal retient la température, le Néo doré – tout comme son homologue en finition inox – pesera sur votre peau comme un kilo de caviar frais, ou comme la main chaleureuse d'un inconnu, selon vos penchants naturels.

De vibrators van Lelo behoren tot de meest populaire ter wereld. Je vindt ze in zowat elke seks- of erotische lifestyleshop en toch heeft het klassieke model Néa met zijn zachte vormen zijn unieke, intieme uitstraling behouden. Dit 18k gouden, klassieke object lijkt wel een miniatuur-Brancusi. Metaal is temperatuurvast en daarom kan deze gouden Néa, evenals de roestvrijstalen staal versie, naar eigen fantasie op je huid aanvoelen als een pondje koele kaviaar of als de warme hand van een onbekende.

Designer: Lelo **Year:** 2003
Webmail: www.lelo.com **Photo:** Katja Kristoferson

Jade bedroom tools

The word "jade" comes from the Spanish *piedra de ijada*, or "loin stone", and it is reputed for its healing properties in that area. Jade is solid as quartz, but can also be very finely shaped (it has been used for everything from axe heads to intricately chiselled tanagras), which means it is ideal for the following purposes: the Ourobouros* cockring, the Lotus flower dildo, and Petite Fesse Lotus flower buttplug.

Le mot « jade » vient de l'espagnol *piedra de ijada*, qui signifie « pierre des flancs », elle est connue pour ses vertus curatives pour la zone rénale. Aussi dure que le quartz, elle peut aussi être très finement polie, ce qui explique ses usages innombrables à travers les siècles- de la tête de hache au tanagra délicatement ciselé. Matériau idéal, donc, pour les objets suivants : le cockring Ouroboros*, le godemiché Fleur de Lotus et le buttplug Petite Fesse Fleur de Lotus.

"Jade" komt van het Spaans "piedra de ijada", of "lendesteen" en staat bekend om zijn helende eigenschappen in die streek. Jade is hard als kwarts, maar kan ook zeer fijn bewerkt worden (het werd voor van alles gebruikt, van bijlen tot complex gebeitelde tanagra's), zodat het ideaal is voor de volgende objecten: De Ourobouros* penisring, de Lotus-dildo en de Petite Fesse Lotus-buttplug.

*A serpent or dragon swallowing its own tail. Ancient symbol of cyclicality, thus very suited to your man's precious parts.
*Serpent ou dragon avalant sa queue. Symbole antique du cycle vital, donc parfaitement adapté aux parties intimes de votre homme.
*Een slang of draak die in zijn eigen staart bijt. Een oud symbool voor het cyclische, dus zeer geschikt voor de edele delen van je man.

Designer: Coco de Mer **Year:** 2005
Webmail: www.coco-de-mer.co.uk **Photo:** Coco de Mer

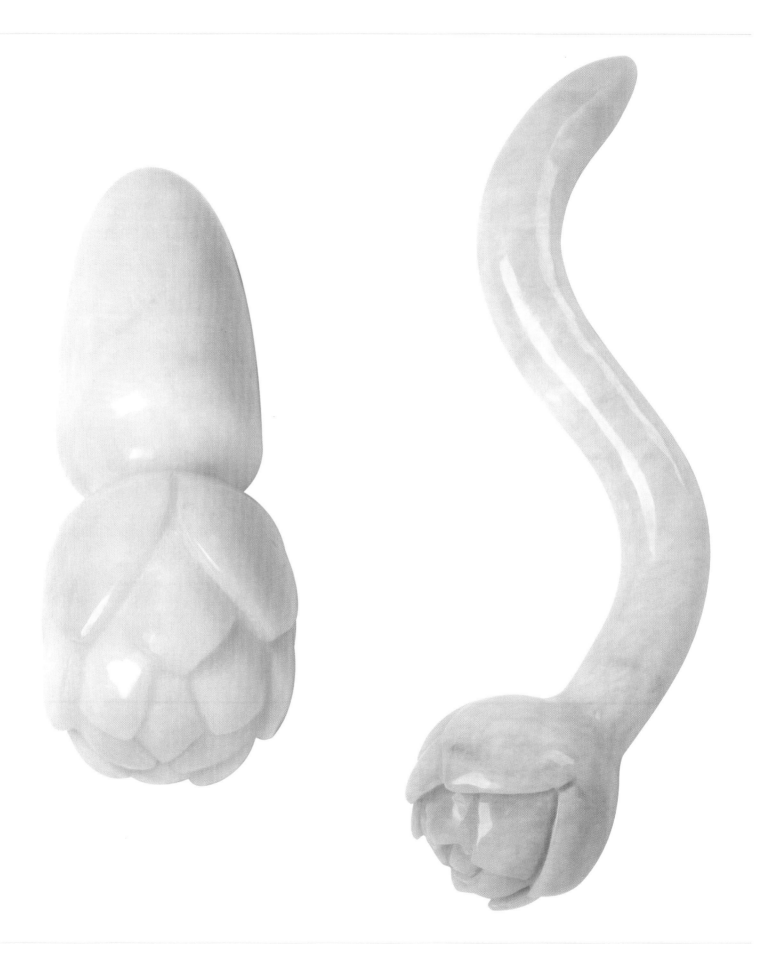

Tip

Part of the *Morte Per* series*, the Tip is a diamond-ended vibrator. Vonhideki concluded that many products are advertised as being extremely beautiful or life enhancing, when in fact it has been proved that they can be harmful to the human body and environment. They decided to take this realization a (long) step further, and apply it literally to product design. Each element of this series is accompanied with (dark) illustrations that place it in context. Morbid indeed, no matter how polished- which is also part of the point.

Tip, un vibromasseur couronné d'un diamant, fait partie de la collection Morte Per* de Vonhideki. Ils sont parti du principe que de nombreux produits sont annoncés comme étant beaux, ou embellissant la vie, alors qu'ils sont notoirement nocifs pour le corps humain et l'environnement. Ils ont donc décidé de pousser ce constat (beaucoup) plus loin en l'appliquant littéralement au design de produit. Chaque élément de la collection s'accompagne d'illustrations (sombres) qui placent l'objet en contexte. Des objets vraiment morbides, aussi raffinés soient-ils – ce qui est justement la thématique qu'ils adressent.

De Tip is een vibrator met diamanten uiteinde en maakt deel uit van de Morte Per reeks*. Vonhideki kwam tot het besluit dat veel producten verkocht worden als uitzonderlijk mooi of levensbelangrijk, terwijl het bewezen is dat ze schadelijk kunnen zijn voor het menselijk lichaam en het milieu. Hij wilde dit besef daarom (ver) doortrekken en letterlijk toepassen op productdesign. Elk element van deze reeks gaat vergezeld van (sombere) illustraties die het een context geven. Inderdaad morbide, hoe verfijnd ook, maar daar gaat het hem nu juist om.

*Italian for "cause of death"
*En italien « cause de la mort »
*Italiaans voor "dood door; doodsoorzaak"

Designer: Vonhideki **Year:** 2005
Webmail: www.vonhideki.com **Photo:** Vonhideki

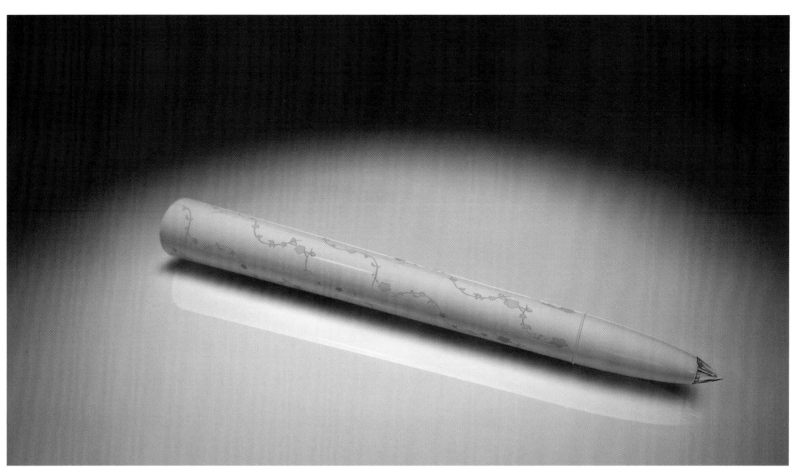

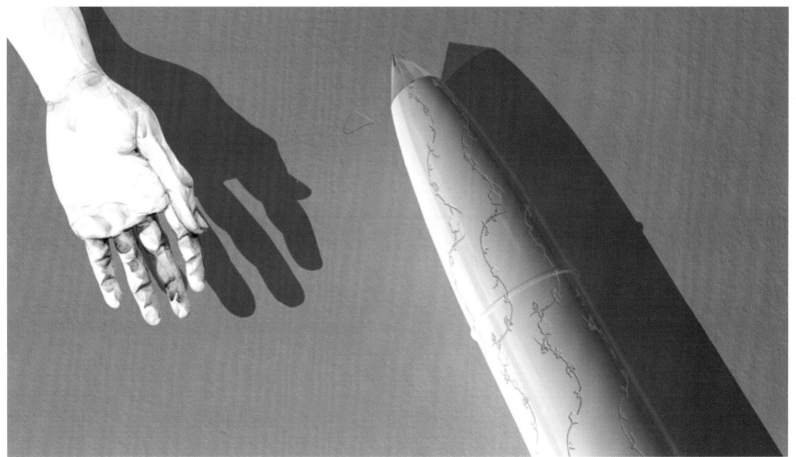

Big Boy cufflinks

A further investigation in her Big Boy series, these cufflinks by Albane Courtière are exceptionally wearable, given their subject matter. The size is small, but they are very sensual, and they all feel different- surprisingly weighty gold ones, super shiny and light silver ones, and delicate glass ones. They make this sweet tinkling sound when swirled in your hand... A straight man could wear them, but why would he need three penises? We imagine them on straight girls and gay men, smiling down at their wrists, each one for their own reasons.

Nouvelle exploration dans la série Big Boy d'Albane Courtière, ces boutons de manchette sont remarquablement portables si l'on considère ce qu'ils représentent. De petits objets, mais très sensuels et tous différents: les boutons en or sont étonnamment lourds, ceux d'argent sont aussi étincelants que légers, et ceux de verre sont d'une grande délicatesse. Manipulés au creux de la main, ils produisent un délicieux tintement... Ils peuvent êtres portés par un hétéro, mais pourquoi diable aurait-il besoin de trois pénis? On les imagine mieux sur une fille hétéro ou un homo, contemplant ses poignets avec un sourire – chacun ses raisons.

Albane Courtière maakte deze manchetknopen binnen haar Big Boy-reeks. Gezien hun thema zijn ze zeer draagbaar. Ze zijn klein maar erg sensueel en voelen allemaal verschillend aan: in verrassend zwaar goud, buitengewoon glanzend, licht zilver en fragiel glas. Ze tinkelen ook zo lief als je er in je hand mee speelt. Een heteroman zou ze kunnen dragen, maar waar heeft hij drie penissen voor nodig? We zien ze eerder op heteromeisjes en mannelijke homo's, die dan naar hun polsen kunnen glimlachen, zij het om verschillende redenen.

Designer: Albane Courtière **Year:** 2006
Webmail: www.albanecourtiere.com **Photo:** Serge Anton

Condom Box

This is a completely different take on the condom box. Romantic, engraved, set with precious stones, the rest of your attire better live up to this item should you whip it out- it takes a particular kind of person to pull it off. Naturally, one of Lorenz Baümer's main creative turn-ons is to make custom jewellery for people with whom he feels mutual interest. Sexy without being vulgar, this gold-plated, diamond and garnet item is definitely bling, but in a Maharajah meets Cupid sort of way.

Voici une déclinaison originale de la boîte à préservatifs, romantique, gravée et incrustée de pierres précieuses. Si vous dégainez cet objet, vous avez tout intérêt à ce que le reste de votre attirail soit à la hauteur, ce qui ne sera pas donné à tout le monde. C'est naturel, l'une des principales motivations créatrices de Lorenz Baümer est de réaliser des bijoux sur mesure pour des personnes avec qui il ressent une affinité. Sexy sans être vulgaire, cette boîte plaquée or, incrustée de diamants et de grenats, est résolument « bling », mais d'une façon quelque peu innocente – ou quand un maharadjah rencontre Cupidon –...

Dit is een heel andere kijk op de condoomdoos. Je kunt je kleding maar beter aanpassen aan dit romantische, gegraveerde en met edelstenen bezette doosje als je van plan bent het tevoorschijn te halen. Dit is niet voor iedereen weggelegd. Iets dat Lorenz Baümer's creatieve brein doet warmlopen is customjuwelen maken voor personen waar hij een wederzijdse interesse bij voelt. Dit vergulde, met diamanten en granaten bezette item springt beslist in het oog, maar dan in de stijl van "Maharaja meets Cupido".

Designer: Lorenz Baümer **Year:** 2004
Webmail: www.lorenzbaumer.com **Photo:** Lorenz Baümer

Little Something, "Fu*k Limited"

Jimmyjane got together with Citizen:Citizen* to make this limited edition version of their ultra-compact, ultra decadent gold or stainless steel Little Somethings. Shown here along Jimmyjane's own platinum version, they look like they could be Midas' or P-Diddy's cigar holders... cigars... forever changed after a cold, cold winter at the White House 1998... Speaking of which, the Little Something can be chilled or heated.

Jimmyjane s'est associé à Citizen:Citizen* pour produire cette édition limitée de son Little Something, un vibromasseur ultra-compact et ultra décadent disponible en finition or ou inox. Présenté aux côtés de la version en platine de Jimmyjane, on dirait l'étui à cigares de Midas ou de P-Diddy... le cigare... transformé à tout jamais après un hiver glacial de 1998 à la Maison-Blanche... À propos, Little Something peut être congelé, ou chauffé.

Jimmyjane maakte samen met Citizen:Citizen* deze versie in beperkte oplage van hun ultra-compacte, ultra-decadente Little Somethings, verkrijgbaar in goud of roestvrij staal. Hier tonen we de platinum versie van Jimmyjane. Ze zien er uit als mogelijke Midas of P-Diddy sigaarhulzen... sigaren... waren nooit meer hetzelfde na die koude, koude winter in het Witte Huis in 1998... Trouwens, de Little Something kan gekoeld of verwarmd gebruikt worden.

*Citizen:Citizen provide provocative, boundary-blurring design, often critical of their main demographic (barefaced, big city hipsters).
*Citizen:Citizen agence de design aimant provoquer et brouiller les cartes, souvent critique de son propre marché (jeunes citadins éhontément branchés).
*Citizen:Citizen staat voor uitdagend, grensverleggend design, vaak kritisch voor hun grootste doelgroep (stadshippies zonder baard).

Designer: Jimmyjane & Citizen:Citizen **Year:** 2007
Webmail: www.jimmyjane.com **Photo:** Jimmyjane

Encore

Lorenz Baümer associated himself with Patrick Bailly-Maître-Grand to produce these daguerreotyped watches. This ancient technique is completely in keeping with the spirit of the watch: the daguerreotype is an early type of photograph in which the image is exposed directly onto a mirror-polished silver surface*. Baümer's perfectionism, love of materials, and strong sense of individuality are all reflected in these creations, not for the meek.

Lorenz Baümer s'est associé à Patrick Bailly-Maître-Grand pour produire ses montres-daguerréotypes. Parfaitement conforme à l'esprit de la montre, le daguerréotype est un ancien procédé photographique par lequel l'image est fixée directement sur une surface d'argent soigneusement polie*. Le perfectionnisme, l'amour des beaux matériaux et le sens de l'individualité dont fait preuve Baümer se reflètent au travers de ses créations, qui s'adressent aux personnalités bien affirmées.

Voor deze daguerreotype horloges werkte Lorenz Baümer samen met Patrick Bailly-Maître-Grand. Deze oude techniek past helemaal bij de spirit van het horloge: de daguerreotype is een vroege vorm van fotografie, waarbij het beeld rechtstreeks op een spiegelend zilveren oppervlak geprojecteerd wordt*. Het perfectionisme, de liefde voor materialen en de sterke individualiteitszin van Baümer zijn allemaal aanwezig in deze creaties. Niet voor meelopers.

*It is a direct positive image-making process with no "negative" original.
*Ce procédé crée une image en positif, sans produire de négatif original.
*Een proces dat direct met positieve beelden werkt, zonder negatieven.

Designer: Lorenz Baümer **Year:** 2004
Webmail: www.lorenzbaumer.com **Photo:** Lorenz Baümer